ACHIEVING

Level-Next

By Gaining Competitive Advantage in the Modern Business Landscape

Dr. Kaustubh Medhekar

ACHIEVING LEVEL-NEXT

Sakal Media Pvt. Ltd.
595, Budhwar Peth,
Pune – 411002, India

www.sakalpublications.com
sakalprakashan@esakal.com

First Edition: November 2024

ISBN No.: 978-93-48048-29-5

Edited by: Yogita Vaidya
Cover Design: Sakal Publications
Typesetting: MAP Systems, Bengaluru

Printed in India by Sakal Media Pvt. Ltd.

Contents

Part I: Concepts of Strategic Management

Part II: Unfolding the Strategic Process

Part III: Exploring Differentiators

List of Figures and Tables

Foreword

Discourses and teachings on strategy have been sought after for centuries. From Machiavelli's *The Art of War* and *The Prince* and Chanakya's *Arthashastra* to modern-day theories, entrepreneurs, managers, and students of strategy have a wealth of information at their fingertips. Yet, despite the availability of tools, techniques, tricks, and tips, what spurs an organization to reach new heights, especially in the modern competitive business landscape?

I appreciate this opportunity to introduce Kaustubh Medhekar's debut book, Achieving 'Level-Next' by Gaining Competitive Advantage in the Modern Business Landscape.

Drawing on his own research, consulting, mentoring, and experience in business strategy, leadership, and finance, Kaustubh tackles these difficult but critical issues. It is his ardent endeavor that learners and practitioners of this guide achieve long-term value in their businesses, focus on important goals, and ascend to the next level while taking new opportunities in their stride.

Kaustubh's recommendations resonate with the journey of many successful organizations—reaching milestones, becoming technologically self-reliant, overcoming setbacks, changing course, tapping into opportunities, and marshaling resources to get far ahead.

Difficulty and misfortune are inevitable and par for the course. Right things could be done at the wrong time or in the wrong place. The best-laid plans made with the noblest of intentions and executed impeccably may still not deliver the results you hoped for. Kaustubh's recommendations on handling the ever-changing VUCA business environment, building winning teams, drawing a dependable strategy, and deploying impactful differentiators are a blueprint to hone an organization's competitive advantage. His suggestions draw on the wisdom of traditional and modern theories, suitably adapting them for the Indian scenario and contemporary volatile markets.

I congratulate Kaustubh on this essential handbook. I also wish readers the very best as they chart new strategies like war generals, with new zeal. All the best, and I hope to see more entrepreneurs and intrapreneurs utilize their talent, skills, and luck to forge ahead.

Dr. Pramod Chaudhari
Executive Chairman
Praj Industries Ltd.

Preface

The quest for Competitive Advantage is unique for each company. This book is meant for SME entrepreneurs to grow their businesses more successfully and quickly. The reader would get enlightened to appreciate what keeps great companies winning year after year, even when yesterday's most hyped businesses failed despite having comparable socio-economic conditions.

The book can serve as an ideal reference book for management students and academicians to learn the concept of Competitive Advantage. The book further explains how this powerful concept is applied in shaping the Strategic Management Process and how it gets implemented to achieve a sustained competitive advantage, in modern-day businesses.

Throughout the book, I have followed a live example of the Premium Transmission Ltd. (PTL) company, illustrating their numbers, and the actual outcome/result that the company obtained after the successful completion of each stage in the Strategic Process. Lastly, the book illustrates impactful differentiators deployed by successful Indian companies in improving their profitability and generating growth.

This book has unearthed the pragmatic flowchart of events to plan a strategic path with valuable lessons. It includes practical assignments needed in shaping your own Winning Team, and for following strategies to achieve "Level-Next."

Dr. Kaustubh Medhekar

Acknowledgments

The thinking set out and the suggestions made in this book have been influenced by my doctoral research work on successful companies. Practical problems faced by companies and pragmatic solutions developed by me, while providing "**ConsultMent**" to SMEs, also gave me valuable insights on the subject.

But for the help of my Executive MBA students, it would have been impossible to get actual data on deployed differentiators of some of the successful Indian companies. I am thankful to the management of Premium Transmission Ltd., (PTL), for allowing me to publish their internal process. I am also thankful to Prof. Kulkarni who was associated with me in ConsultMent assignments at PTL.

I am grateful for the inspiration provided by the Late Mr. P. P. Chhabria and Mr. Pramod Chaudhari for this book. I am privileged and grateful to have had personal interactions and deliberations with some of the successful first-generation entrepreneurs, and their valuable suggestions immensely benefited me in shaping my ideas while writing this book.

Introduction

India has launched the "Make in India" campaign to enhance Business Growth. To create substantial jobs and wealth, for the national economy, for the local community, and for the entrepreneurs themselves, businesses not only need to be started, they also need to survive and grow. The SME sector plays a vital role in the growth of India and as of date contributes almost 40% of the gross industrial value added (GVA) in the Indian economy.

Covid19 pandemic has opened up unprecedented opportunities for Indian manufacturing, supply-chain companies, and the service sector. Many Japanese, American, and European companies have indicated their interest in shifting their business base out of China. India under democracy with a large pool of skilled and young population can certainly make use of this situation and attract a large portion of businesses. Entrepreneurs in India must act fast and learn how to run a business competitively.

Business survival and business growth are linked. Professor David Storey, in his comprehensive 1994 book *Understanding the Small Business Sector*, noted that "The fundamental characteristic, other than size per se, which distinguishes small firms from large is their higher probability of ceasing to trade." This means bigger businesses are more likely to survive as they are in a better position to survive the loss of key customers or loss of a key member of staff, and have a wider range of products/ services and more financial strength, which allows them to ride out drops in demand and the ups and downs of the economic cycle.

Growing a business is not easy, particularly for companies in developing countries like India. In reality, the challenges of growing a business are often even more difficult to overcome than the challenges of starting a business. Entrepreneurs with aspirations to grow have to learn to manage and lead the business. They face complex business scenarios and global competition. They need to find, retain, and motivate other people to share the increased workload, and they need to continue to invest in business growth.

Business success depends on real-time monitoring, performance measurement, and rapid problem resolution. This is becoming an increasingly critical element of both strategy formulation and operational execution. Most companies today are forced by competitive pressures to develop and adjust strategies almost continuously. It is imperative to become proactive and get stronger as business becomes more global and threats increase.

(Although the data of companies used in the book is dated, the quantities and amounts illustrated are useful to understand the concepts.)

Part I
Concepts of Strategic Management

Part 1 introduces you, the learners, to the rapidly changing scenario of the business landscape and traces the evolution and development of the concept of **Competitive Advantage** to help you understand how to grow your business.

Chapter 1

Dynamic Business Landscape of Indian Companies

The decade of the nineties witnessed consolidation and rationalization in the industry. During the same time, economic reforms were shaping the country. The post-globalization phase 1991 onward brought out the best in the industry, which highlighted the need for optimizing manpower and costs, putting in quality systems, increasing cross-segment exposure, and strategizing processes. This led to the growth of SMEs as a sector. Eventually, some of the SMEs (that survived the economic recession of 1995-98) have grown and have a global presence. However, others were left behind and perished.

India is fast moving out of low-cost production. Managers often face the dilemma of whether to focus on long-term or short-term objectives. Focusing only on short-term strategies blurs the shareholder's value in the distant horizon. Focusing only on the long-term diminishes the company's ability for sustained internal generation. Thus, executives face two daunting challenges as they strive to create sustainable companies.

1. The genuine need for short-term stewardship can distract managers, even those with the best intentions, from their long-term vision.
2. Defining the long-term strategy and embedding it into today's operations are more complicated than they may seem at first glance. Creating long-term value does not negate the need to tend to the immediate needs of a company. When driving a car, it isn't enough to know the destination (**Competitive Advantage**). You must also be aware of the vehicles around you (**External Environment**), the course of the road and the capability of your car (**Internal Capabilities**), your fuel level (**Strategic Choices**), and other pressing matters (**Implementation**). Additionally, managers also have to do a better job at recognizing the short-term pressures that needlessly interfere with their long-term goals.

In the twenty-first century, business has become hyper-competitive. One needs to look back at the past, absorb and feel the present, and dare to imagine a future. Let us take a pause and look back to see how progress has spaced over the recent years. Overwhelmingly, a majority of all the material goods we use and take for granted have been developed in our lifetime. Maybe today we are already in the next lifetime, fully engulfed by the information wave, aided and controlled by computers and robots, catapulted by technology into the surrounding new, alien, and too-fast world aided by AI (Artificial Intelligence). Look around closely and observe any sector, any product, and you will know that today is different from yesterday. No one can predict how tomorrow will be and why because technology breeds itself. As an entrepreneur, one has to be ready for an ever-changing business world.

The rapidly changing business landscape throws serious challenges, particularly for SMEs. Developmental forces have flattened the world and created multiple new forms and tools for collaborations, and new opportunities, new challenges, and new partners in business. Companies have to stand the ever-accelerating pace of progress and change that impacts all aspects of business. They have to judge how the said factors will impact and transform their business. They have to be watchful about how competition will acquire new forms. Leaders have to keep pace with the ever-changing environment in which their businesses operate. They have to pause, ponder, and proactively take the initiative in knowing what is happening around their business.

Technology aided by suitable management skills has been helping successful companies to grow their top-line (sales) and consistently manage to keep their bottom-line (profit) healthy. Such progressive companies have realized that in the new economy, the critical assets are know-how, creativity, intelligence, and information, whereas in the old economy, land, labor, and capital were considered to be critical. Successful firms seamlessly adopt new ways of doing business and keep progressing. Particularly "Business-to-business" (B2B) companies get little publicity, but their success is no accident. They have discovered patterns of success that have largely gone unnoticed by their unsuccessful competitors and by the industry in general.

The business world is bursting with ideas. Week upon week, countless new trends make the news. Such trends tend to affect both, the way of doing business and the perception of customers about the products they use. Companies have to cope with and differentiate between the changes that are mere novelties and the changes that have an enduring impact. Decide too soon and the company risks investing in a fad. Take action too late and the company may miss the next big thing. The ways of maintaining Competitive Advantage, therefore, are continuously evolving and remain in a paradigm state. Differentiation is known as a high level of discriminator; however, which differentiators to deploy for a company's success is not easy to comprehend.

•••

Chapter 2

Evolution of the Theory of Competitive Advantage

This chapter covers the period from the 1970s when strategic thinking in business started with the concept of Portfolio Planning. In the 1980s, the theory of Competitive Advantage emerged and became popular with researchers who further evolved the understanding of Business Strategy.

The next four decades saw further development of the various dimensions of the concept of Competitive Advantage, enriched by researchers. It is advisable for a keen strategy learner to understand the basic principles shaping strategy and assimilate the gradual development of the powerful concept of Competitive Advantage. This would prepare entrepreneurs to think broadly and deeply at the same time and effectively shape suitable strategies in their own company.

Portfolio Planning

General Electric Company's (GE) corporate structure had 200 profit centers and 145 departments arranged around 10 group companies. McKinsey, GE's consultants, were unable to define the boundaries of these units in terms of financial controls. McKinsey's study recommended a formal strategic planning system that would divide the company into strategic business units (SBUs). The said consultants suggested following a nine-block matrix to screen the industry attractiveness and competitive position in the given industry.

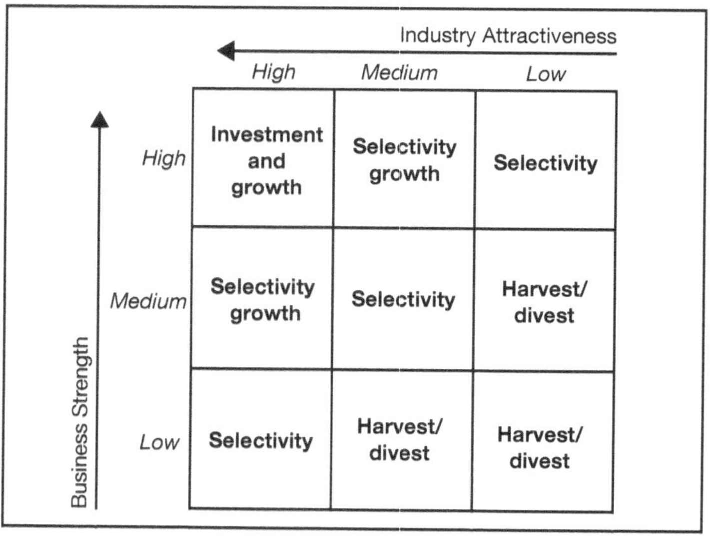

Fig. 1 GE / McKinsey Nine-Block Matrix

This methodology came to be known as "Portfolio Planning" and enabled one to calculate each SBU's results in terms of its costs and other performance yardsticks. It made it possible to sort out winners and losers, setting priorities and husbanding capital. Eventually, Portfolio Planning gave executives an excuse to get rid of underperforming business units and direct more resources/funds to star performers.

However, in the 1980s, the technique of resource allocation based on Portfolio Planning was challenged since this technique relied on historical data, and it was assumed that financial capital was the only scarce resource. Fred Gluck, head of McKinsey's strategic management practice, proposed those successful companies' strategies should gradually progress from static analysis to dynamic analysis, through the four stages stated below.

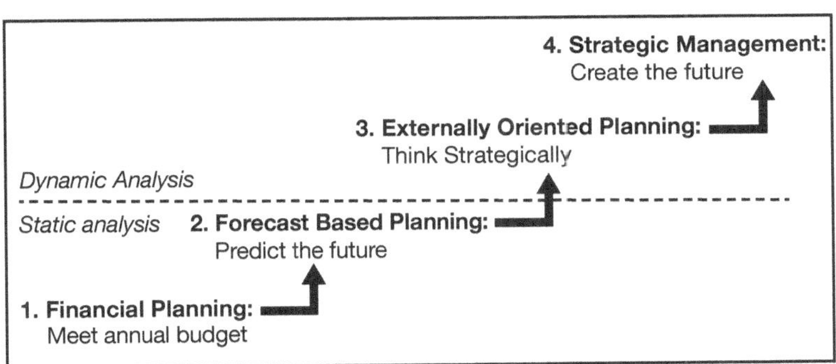

Fig. 2 Stages in Strategic Management

The said Four Stages Strategy avoided heavy dependence on the "packaged techniques" suggested under Portfolio Management, which frequently resulted in tightening up or fine-tuning only the current initiatives within the traditionally configured businesses.

The Four Stages Strategy involves grappling with increasing levels of dynamism, multidimensionality, and uncertainty and therefore becomes less amenable to routine quantitative analysis. However, careful analysis of two basic dimensions of "industry attractiveness and competitive position," prescribed under Portfolio Planning, continued to have a lasting influence on the strategist community.

Five Forces Framework for Industry Analysis

The Five Forces Framework developed by Professor Michael Porter enables companies to map the Business Landscape in which they operate. The five forces are as follows:

- Competitors in your own industry
- Suppliers with bargaining power with your company
- Substitute products to your own along with their pricing
- Bargaining power of the buyers of your products/services, and
- New entrants in your line of business

The Five Forces Framework (table below) states the different threats affecting your company. The listed factors and their ingredients constantly impact your business model and your business edge vis-à-vis competitors in the industry in which you operate. The knowledge and assessment of the said Five Forces would enable you to map your business landscape and prepare you for the next stage of dynamic thinking to plan your strategy. A business landscape maps each business strategy's elevation according to its economic profitability.

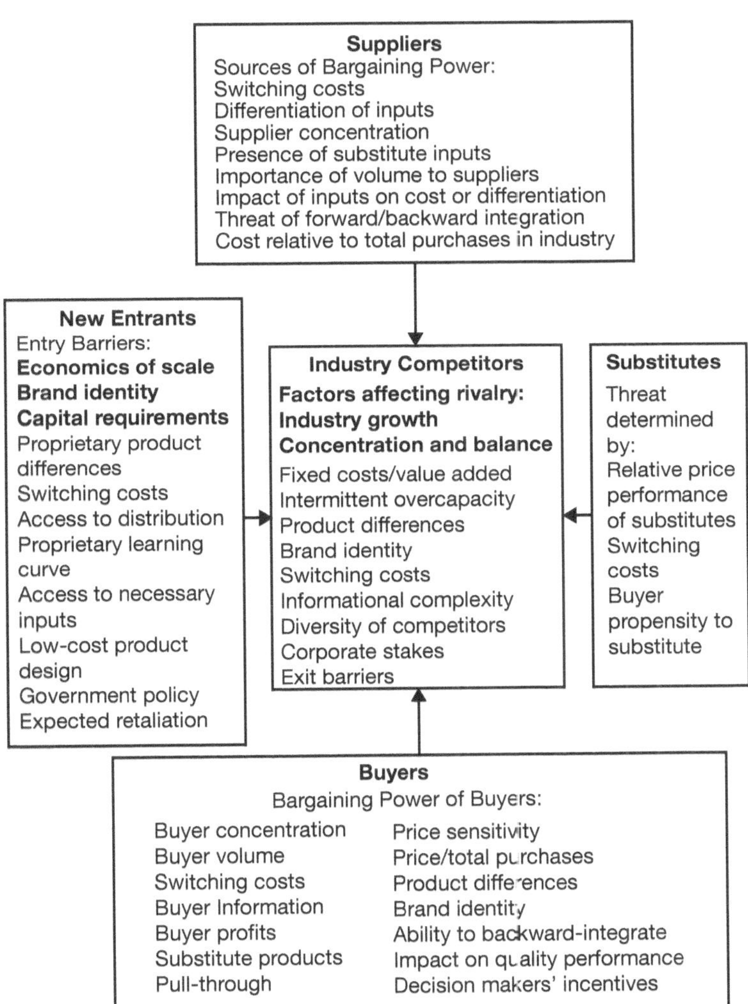

Fig. 3 The Five Forces Framework

(Source: Pankaj Ghemawat: Strategy and the Business Landscape)

Business Mapping Process

After assessing the said threats, the CEO should move to strategic planning and action for effectively mapping the business landscape for his company. The six-step process includes the following steps:

(A) Gathering relevant information from industry studies, annual reports, government sources, business directories, conferences, and others (Dun & Bradstreet)

(B) Drawing boundaries by taking an inside-out approach. Start with the business's served market, but include unserved segments under the control of competitors. This enables the CEO to focus on the horizontal scope across product markets

(C) Identifying Groups of Players such as direct competitors, potential entrants, substitute products, complementing products, buyers, and suppliers

(D) Understanding group-level bargaining power

(E) Thinking dynamically, and finally,

(F) Shaping the business landscape

Dynamic Thinking

This analysis suggests the potential usefulness of long-term dynamics. It is the futuristic understanding of how the landscape "will be" in next three to five years (short-term) and the next ten years (long-term). Consider dynamics as market growth, the evolution of buyer needs, the rate of product and process innovation, a change in the scale to remain competitive, changes in input cost, and exchange rate.

Let us consider the example of a pharmaceutical company in India, planning its long-term strategic agenda. Such a company must consider the following future trends:

- Increased drug discovery by a biotechnology specialist, and the possibility of its competitors outsourcing their new drug discovery to such a specialist.
- Increased dependence by customers on branded companies, and possible mergers of such companies or their new entry in the Indian market.
- Increasing threat from generic manufacturers and their imitative trend.
- Imports from countries producing cheaper drugs and direct to consumer suppliers.

Common dynamics and their interdependence in mapping the Business Landscape is presented in a tabular form below for greater understanding of the different variables impacting the product's life cycle dynamics.

The above discussion was on macro-analysis at the level of the business landscape. Based on these broad guidelines, CEOs have to do a micro-analysis for shaping their own Business Landscape to formulate suitable strategic action.

The "Five Forces Framework" and "Landscape Analysis" assist in shaping meaningful SWOT (Strengths, Weaknesses, Opportunities, and Threats) analysis to formulate suitable business actions to face competition.

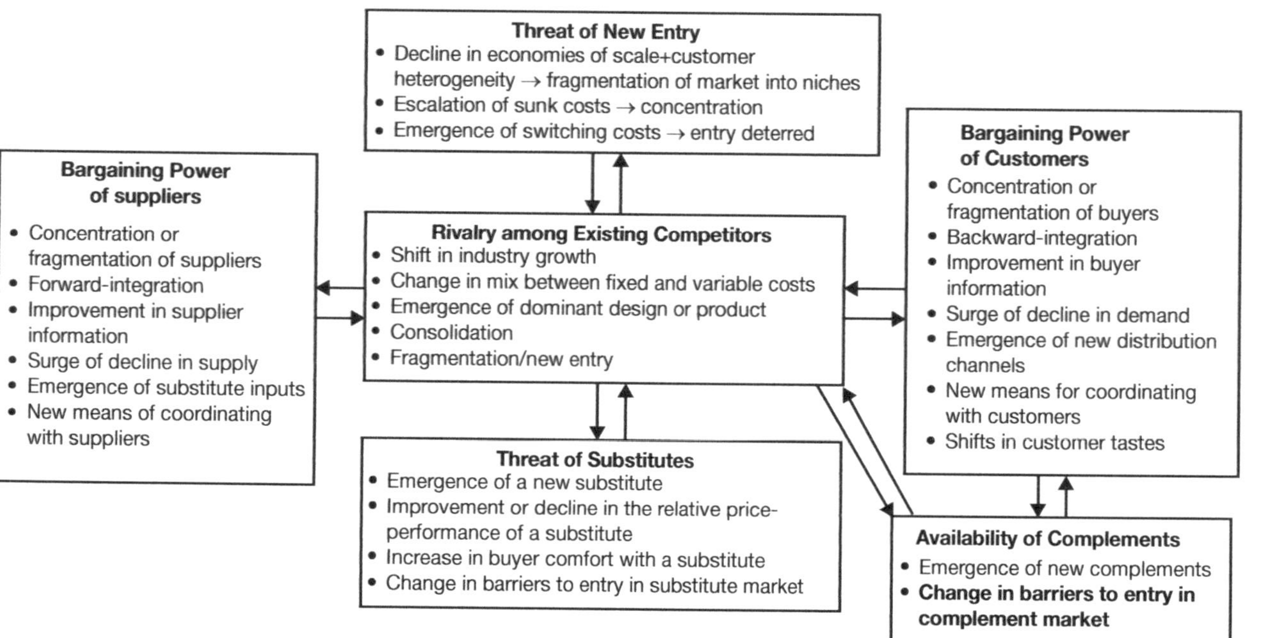

Fig. 4 Mapping the Business Landscape

(Source: Pankaj Ghemawat: Strategy and the Business Landscape)

The Theory of Competitive Advantage

In the mid-1980s, Professor Michael Porter developed the theory and concept of "Generic Competitive Advantage." The original theory and concept of Competitive Advantage had three parts:

(a)   Select an attractive industry.

(b)   Get competitive advantage through cost leadership & product differentiation.

(c)   Develop value chains.

Professor Porter, in 1985, found that effective application of the said factors does contribute to success in business. Success was measured by performance categories such as "Below Average, Average, and Above Average." In other words, Competitive Advantage is a condition that puts a company in a superior position in business as compared to its rivals.

Enriching the concept of Competitive Advantage

The theory of Competitive Advantage was well received among international researchers, and over the past four decades, many scholars have worked extensively on enriching this powerful concept. Examining the dimensions and interpretations developed by various researchers in enhancing the understanding of the concept of Competitive Advantage would perhaps be the best way to begin the study of shaping business strategy.

(1)   In 1988, Professor E. S. Weber and Benn's research on neglected elements in the Decision Support System (DSS) in business advocated developing the full range of problem-solving events: problem finding - problem representation

- information surveillance - solution generation - and evaluation. DSSs are designed for decision makers who, having identified critical issues, modeled the important problems, amassed relevant information, and generated appropriate ideas to choose the effective course of action.

(2) Innovation requires talent, ingenuity, and knowledge, but the caution is that if diligence, persistence, and commitment are lacking, organizations won't succeed in the business of innovation. Management guru Peter Drucker, in 1988, found that there should be simple, focused solutions to real problems and not grandiose ideas.

(3) Professor P. Senge, 1990, researched on Organizational Learning. It was found that learning organizations facilitate the learning of their members and continuously transform to face emerging challenges. To remain competitive in the business environment, firms must be disciplined towards Personal Mastery, System's Thinking, Mental Models, Team Learning, and Shared Vision.

(4) Professor K. Ohmae, in 1991, analyzed the mind of a strategist and claimed that all pioneers of new industries have the God-given gift of looking ahead and appointing reliable and efficient employees to attain common goals.

(5) Professor Kalpan Robert and Norton David of Harvard Business School introduced the Key Performance Measurement (KPI) framework that added non-financial measures to traditional financial metrics to give a "balanced" view of organizational performance. (KPIs: customer satisfaction, product quality, market share, productivity, service quality, and core competencies.) The KPI framework is a strategic planning and management

system that is used extensively in business and industry worldwide to align business activities to the vision and strategy of the organization, improve external and internal communications and monitor organizational performance against strategic goals. The typical KPI process published in the Harvard Business Review (HBR) in 1996 is presented below.

Fig. 5 The KPI Process

(6)   Management guru C. K. Prahalad and G. Hamel, in 1997, found that Core Competencies are generated through collective learning in the organization, especially how to coordinate diverse production skills and integrate multiple schemes of technologies. The recognition and development of core competencies rely on communication and cooperation across traditional organizational boundaries. The authors recommended three conditions for identifying core competencies:

(a) It must have the potential to form the basis for entry into new product markets.

(b) It must make a significant contribution to the customer's perceived value.

(c) It should be difficult for competitors to imitate.

The concept of Core Competencies was researched for "its adaptation" by large multinational companies – GTE (US) and NEC (Japan), in formulating their growth strategies. NEC excelled and became the industry leader because it conceived itself in terms of "Core Competencies."

(7) Professor Johnson, in 1998, coined the concept of "Benchmarking." Benchmarking is a process for improving performance by constantly identifying, understanding and adapting best practices and processes followed inside and outside the company, and implementing the results. The main emphasis of benchmarking is on improving the given business operation or process by exploiting the "best practices," and not "best performance." A typical benchmarking exercise is a four-stage process involving planning, data collection, data analysis and reporting, and adaptation.

Benchmarking principles were first adapted by Xerox, an American company. By practicing these principles, Xerox reaped rich benefits, *viz.* the number of defects in products reduced by 78%; the service response time was reduced by 27%; inspection time of incoming components reduced to below 5%; inventory cost reduced by two-thirds, and errors in billing reduced from 8.3% to 3.5 %. Xerox could win many prestigious awards like the European Quality Award in 2002. In short, the company achieved competitive advantage by doing their business with less time wastage, lower costs, fewer resources, and better technology.

(8)   Professor J. Pfeffer, and R. Sutton, in their 1999 research, highlighted the importance of maintaining "Simplicity" in corporate Strategic Process, breaking things down into smaller and manageable parts, and having one-to-one discussions, and argued that clarity of the plan at the CEO level is important to business success.

(9)   Professor C. Compbell, in his research paper published in the year 2000, established (by using the Meta-Analysis technique) that the Competitive Advantage theory remains crucial to the study of Strategic Management and tried to establish linkages between the theory and the firm's performance.

(10) Harvard Business School (HBS) published the work done by Professor G. Colarelli and Liefer who found that innovation includes product development, transactions, process, paradigms, and exploration of competencies. "Incremental innovation" emphasizes cost reduction and improvements in existing products. "Radical innovations" include the development of new businesses or product lines – based on new ideas or technologies or substantial cost reduction – that transform the economics of a business and therefore require exploration competencies.

(11) Professor M. Alavi and D. E. Leinder, in 2001, found the importance of "Knowledge Management" in different layers of management structure. Their research analyzed many successful companies and concluded that the upgradation of skills and on-the-job training does help multinational

companies to raise the performance bar at different layers of the organization.

(12) Professor C. Nobes, in 2001, defined various important accounting terminologies such as Top-line, Bottom-line, Net-worth, and others that are internationally used to assess and describe business success in financial terms.

(13) Professor J. C. Collins, in 2001, studied elite firms that made the leap to great results and sustained them for a long period. The findings from such firms revealed that Level 5 leaders (lower ranks) contribute maximum to the profitability. The firm has to transcend the curse of competence, bring in a culture of discipline, practice ethical entrepreneurship, and think differently about the role of technology.

(14) Professor R. Burgelman researched the strategic process of Intel in 2002. Intel had not only survived for three decades but had also thrived in the face of explosive change and upheavals. R. Burgelman documented the key role played by mid-level managers and top managers in finding their way through strategic conundrums and the complex role of the CEO in giving a strategic thrust to shape the future. This research work truly described strategy-in-action and threw light on the importance of quality in strategy-making processes.

(15) Jack Welch, in 2002, found that the company's quest for competitive advantage is framed around five generic competitive strategies: low-cost leadership, differentiation, best-cost provider, focused differentiation, and focused low-cost. The firm complements its choice of basic competitive strategy by deploying various strategic actions such as

strategic alliances, mergers and acquisitions, vertical integration strategies, outsourcing strategies, and offensive and defensive strategies to position itself in the marketplace. He concludes that by adopting such techniques, companies should make winners out of every business they are in and disinvest from the loss-making businesses.

(16) Philips company's successful adaptation of the "Restructuring Exercise" helped them to promote the spirit of "Internal Collaboration" to regain their branding as an innovative company. The company launched a restructuring program called TOP (Towards One Philips). Under this globally launched program, the company developed a customer focus, integrated the innovation base, lowered costs, and promoted collaborations. This changed the mindset and helped the company in attaining market leadership and improved profits.

(17) L. Bossidy, Ram Charan, and C. Burck, in their 2002 research, revealed that a business leader has to know at least the top third of the people, get down to where the action is by talking to people, establish a personal connection, be open to boundary-less thinking, be open for options that differ from his own, and finally, practice and lead the honest, inclusive dialogues that bring reality into the open. The CEO has to put a high premium on getting things done, winning and attracting the very best and the most diverse talent, and getting the strategy process right for long-term success.

(18) Canon (India), then a loss-making company, based on market analysis and foreseeing future trends in customer preferences, launched a massive restructuring exercise. Restructuring the organizational setup helped them

revamp the company's products, brand building, sales, and distribution channels, and consumer service strategies to turn the corner and become profitable.

(19) The collection of research studies conducted by Harvard Business School's professors, in 2003, found that innovative firms do stay ahead of the curve, but innovation alone is not sufficient to gain Competitive Advantage. Companies must ultimately turn those ideas into profits. Prof. A. Pearson found that consistent innovation, a key to market leadership, can be achieved by the CEO's belief, encouragement to innovation, knowledge of competitive dynamics of the company's business, determination to leverage existing strength, and to "go for it" when the idea is fully developed. Lord Keynes's research suggested that a powerful idea must have the potential to be translated into practice. T. Levitt, Professor Emeritus at Harvard Business School, argued that large companies facilitate innovation. Only the organizational insider – the apparent conformist has the practical intelligence to overcome bureaucratic impediments and bring a good idea to fruitful conclusion. Peter Drucker wrote: Define a problem and then solve it. Allow people to experiment not only about products but also about customer service, business models and networking and put emphasis on pure science just as you put emphasis on the markets.

(20) The research of B. N. Anand (HBS Case # N2-704-438, 2004) deals with successful "Implementation Strategies" adopted by Random House (a publication company), in gaining and sustaining "Market Share" and "Profit Margin" by consolidating along with market demands and changing

customer preferences. Assessing industry trends, detailing on industry economics, merging with a competitor, altering the organization structure, and integrating backward to "paper production" proved effective in gaining competitive advantage.

(21) Findings of A. S. Groves Research, in 2004, suggest that strategic inflection points can be caused by technology upgradation by competitors and the way business is conducted (transitional changes). It was found that such changes strike not only the margin but also the very foundation/existence of the business.

(22) This research paper discussed the barriers of performance within the Management Team, and how to overcome them to improve performance. The major barriers are the mission not being clear, lack of empowerment, a member being a poor fit for his role, no upgradation of skillsets, and the inability to transform member conflict into synergy. To perform effectively, a team needs to operate as a unified group and within a large environment with a possibly different culture than that which develops inside the team.

(23) J. Barney and W. S. Hesterly, in 2006, coined the concept of Resource-Based View (RBV). RBV is a model of a firm's performance that focuses on the resources and capabilities controlled by a firm as sources of competitive management. In the "resource-based theory," the relevance and role of company resources and competitive strengths need to be comprehensively integrated in crafting the firm's strategies. A firm's strategy must be matched with both its external market circumstances and its internal resources and competitive capabilities. Moreover, various aspects of

executing strategies have a strong resource-based perspective that encompasses many tasks of assembling intellectual capital and building core competencies and competitive capabilities that are critical to successful strategy execution and operating excellence.

(24) Harvard Business Publication (HBP), in 2006, published research that deals with creating "Blue Oceans" or how to create an uncontested "Marketplace" and make competition irrelevant.

(25) S. Bagchi, in 2006, wrote "The High Performance Entrepreneur: Golden Rules for Success in Today's World." In today's competitive business world, the golden rules of success were found in personal and team characteristics – persistence, integrity, passion, and sacrifice – that result in high-performance entrepreneurship. Successful entrepreneurs need to – commence with sensing the right opportunity, choose suitable teams, have business DNA in them with clarity of vision and mission, carefully write business plans, choose the right investors, not only get good people but also key executives, build a process-focused organization, select and maintain good customers, manage their resources, build their brand, have the emergence and willingness to change, and develop the ability to manage adversity.

(26) Business Process Management (BPM), according to H. Smith and P. Fingar, (2006), enables firms to solve complex problems and contribute to corporate sustainability, innovation, and growth. For "managing the change," organizations and employees have to change themselves to better understand customer needs, technology, individuals in the team, and society. BPM provides the capability to

improve the efficiency of value chain partners, systems, ERP, and time-to-market concepts and reduces the cycle-time between management intent and execution.

(27) P. Chaudhari, in 2008, wrote an autobiography of a successful technocrat, who has grown his business with the active help and involvement of his intrapreneurs (dedicated and committed employees) to churn out continuous competitive advantage and sustained growth by creating and converting innovative ideas into profits.

(28) H. E. Gardner's research, in 2009, deals with how people learn, create, lead, and change the minds of others. The world of the future will demand capacities that until now have been mere options. He named five cognitive abilities that will command a premium in the future. They are a Disciplined mind, a Synthesizing mind, a Creative mind, a Respectful mind, and an Ethical mind.

(29) The research of Per Davidsson & others, 2010, is on the conceptual and empirical complexity of the "Firm Growth" phenomenon. Recognizing the heterogeneity that exists in the firm's growth, and growth being a multidimensional phenomenon, authors, however, felt that more research is required in constructing appropriate samples and measures.

(30) In the book, "Knowledge Innovation: Strategic Management as Practice," Mitsuru Kodama describes how strategic communities (SC) in complex organizations serve as catalysts for knowledge innovation in highly competitive environments. Through detailed case studies, he demonstrated how Japanese companies in the telecommunications and related fields have turned traditional organizational lines

inside out, which has resulted in breakthroughs in new technologies and products.

(31) In G. C. Reid, 2007, a new kind of "micro-micro" research, applying rigorous methods from economics, accounting, and finance was considered by various authors to gain a deeper understanding of micro-firms, by examining their performance, hierarchy, flexibility in responding to market conditions and information techniques.

(32) In Burke & others, 2008, the authors listed key challenges for "Owner-Managers" of small firms to achieve sustained and profitable growth: Planning vacuum, muddled marketing, mismanaged change, wrong objectives, lack of time management, and poor financial controls.

(33) L. Hobbs, 2008 – Effective strategy is the key to successful management, which connects otherwise disparate management efforts by coordinating them with an overall strategy. This research elaborated on how strategic DNA is cultivated, nurtured, and implemented in modern organizations.

(34) A. Gaba, R. Hogarth, and Makridakis, 2008 – This research dealt with the importance of the "role of forecasting" after the global recession where "Triple-A" became "subprime" and "toxic." The authors claimed there are plenty of sophisticated models that can fit past data, but in an uncertain world, one has to forecast realistically, assess the trends, and consider extreme events occurring to avoid many surprises in making business decisions.

(35) In M. Moldoveanu and R. Martin, 2009, the researchers analyzed how the minds of successful businessmen work and coined them "Diaminds." Such minds have the ability to flip between different modes of thinking while dealing

with a greater range of ambiguous and complex situations. They could flip between thinking deeply and broadly at the same time. The authors found that the quest for successful intelligence has proved to be elusive for behavioral scientists. IQ, EQ, MQ, and many more, coupled with presumably stable and measurable personality traits like conscientiousness, extroversions, and even neuroticism, can explain only 25-30% of the variance in outcomes. The authors found in their research that such a successful businessman's "Diamind" was not limited to seeing objects or phenomena in different ways, but also did its thinking in different ways.

(36) S. Snyder, P. Shoemaker, and G. Day (2009) – The periphery – that fuzzy zone at the edge of the organization's focus – is where early signals of both threats and opportunities are first sensed. "Peripheral Vision" provides valuable warnings and enables vigilant leaders to adopt an inquisitive approach to strategy that alerts them to possible changes. In an interconnected world, vigilant organizations have been employing networks to compete effectively by monitoring other industries, remote markets, new research, and tangential data, which entails much more than sensing incipient changes. It is also about knowing where to look for clues, how to interpret weak signals, and how to act when signals are still ambiguous. Research listed four ways to leverage networks and tap into the knowledge and insights of the periphery. They are sharing intelligence, external scanning, customized insights, and open innovation.

(37) P. Ghemawat and Others, 2009 – The authors developed a strategy to suit Business Landscapes through a process of gathering information, drawing boundaries, identifying

competitors, understanding group-level bargaining power, thinking dynamically and shaping the business landscape to create and sustain Competitive Advantage.

(38) M. Kupp, J. Reckhenrich and J. Anderson, 2010 – This research found that global CEOs identified "creativity" as the most important leadership competency for firms seeking competitive advantage in the contemporary business world. Such leaders are able to shape organizations according to the complex needs of modern businesses. Fostering creativity has two dimensions – "individual" and "collective."

(39) IBM's research paper, 2010 – The research is about the quest for creativity and capitalizing on the complexity of business. To promote sustained innovation, intermediaries must be created who will visualize new opportunities synthesized from the insight of technologies provided by several companies and give them to the organization needing them, for a fee.

(40) McKinsey & Co, 2009 – In their research, the leading management consultants found that differentiated products and a strong brand scored 2.6 points on their Total Returns to Shareholders (TRS) index, whereas non-differentiated product companies that do not have an established brand scored negative 6.2 points, a difference of 365 percent.

(41) Revista Academiei Fortelor published research on Strategic Human Resources Management in the Maritime Knowledge-based Organization in their Vol.15, Issue 1. The authors found that strategic human resource management is the process of linking the function of human resources and the managerial process, requiring human resource policies and practices with the strategic objectives of the organization. (Blagovest and others, March 2010).

(42) Budapest Management Review published a research paper on Business at the Speed of Light – The Role of Time and Speed on Business Strategy in their Vol. 41, Issue 6. The paper focuses on the importance of the dimensions of time and speed in the world of competitive strategy. In today's global village, businesses struggle with competitors in the industry to achieve sustainable competitive advantage through the creation of economies of scale and/or economies of scope along with achieving economy of time. The paper describes the trends in the area of impact of time and speed on the world of strategy and presents the main parameters that influence the speed of implementation of strategic processes by companies (Morag and others, Jan 2010).

(43) Various, TMTC Journal, 2011 – The Tatas went in for massive structural and philosophical changes around 2000 to adjust to the challenges that came up due to the opening of the Indian economy. The plan to protect their vulnerable stake (TATA Sons's holding of only 3% in TISCO) from global corporate raiders was drafted along with a list of disinvestments from the non-priority sector. The Strategic Planning Process was launched to decide what businesses they wanted to continue; competitive advantage for the group as a whole was chalked out; the company's mission, turnover targets, and growth plans were revised; structural changes were made to get the holding company in conclusive command; a list of businesses was finalized for disinvestment; Tata was promoted as a common brand across different types of businesses; customer and market focus were redefined; and many more steps were taken to take on the global competition.

(44) Sangadieva, Jan-March 2012 – The IG bulletin of the East Siberian State University published an article: Conceptual Bases of Strategic Management and Planning in their journal Vol. 36, Issue 1. The article considered the application of the principles of strategic management and planning process, a variant of process modeling, for regional strategic planning.

(45) A. I. Value Inquiry Book Services in their Vol. 276 published a research paper titled Management, Strategic. The author opined that Strategic Management is a method by which decision-makers structure their ideas on the condition of the management system with its variability limitations and on practical approaches to developing and implementing a strategy. This method is a matrix of complex variables. The deeper and more thoroughly these variables cover the subject, the more practical they are as navigation devices in the ocean of business. (Ageev, 2014).

Summary

This chapter reviewed the historical development and understanding of gaining Competitive Advantage in business, spanning over four decades and revealed the various new trends and concepts, which proved effective in shaping successful business in the contemporary world.

As seen in this chapter, The Competitive Management Theory is continuously evolving and remains in a paradigm state. However, the knowledge of such research work equips entrepreneurs with the agenda of planning and implementing an effective strategy for their own business success.

•••

Part II

Unfolding the Strategic Process

Part II of the book deals with the meaning of Business Strategy and how it should be shaped, how strategic choices are made, how gaps in business are analyzed, how your own Winning Teams should be developed, and how the intended business plan should be practiced and implemented in the company to create sustainable competitive advantage and generate high business growth despite global competition. The stages explained in chapters 3-6 are generic in nature and can be easily understood and deployed in various types of businesses. This suggested methodology has considered a wide range of factors that keep changing in the marketplace.

Strategy in Business

The most inclusive and practical definition of strategy, in my opinion, is offered by Professor Alfred D Chandler. According to him, "Strategy can be defined as the determination of the basic long-term goals and objectives of an enterprise and the adoption of courses of action and the allocation of resources necessary for carrying out those goals."

The characteristics associated with strategic decisions are as follows:

- Strategy deals with long-term (a span of 5-10 years) objectives and the direction of an organization. It includes both organic and inorganic growth/ expansion of an organization.
- Strategic decisions are concerned with the scope of the organization's activities. For example, how many products the company should have, the intended geographical coverage, and other related activities to conceive the company's boundaries.
- A strategy can be seen as a search for the strategic fit with the business environment in which the company operates. This means achieving the correct positioning of the organization, for example, in terms of the extent to which products or services meet identified market needs. This might take the form of a small business trying to find a particular niche in the market or a multinational seeking to buy businesses that have already found successful market positions, leading to gaining an advantage over competitors.
- A strategy includes creating opportunities by building the company's resources and competencies. This is called a resource-based view of strategy, which is concerned with exploiting the strategic capability of a company, in terms of the resources and competencies, to provide competitive advantage and yield new opportunities. For example, a small business may try to change "the rules of the game" in its market to suit

its own capabilities (Dell Computers approaching consumers directly with a thin margin) or a multinational deciding to concentrate only on strong brands in a country.

- Strategic decisions demand an integrated approach to managing the organization. Managers have to cross the functional and operational boundaries to deal with strategic problems and come to an agreement with cross-sectional interest groups to reach the most beneficial option/s.
- Strategic decisions must consider the outside networks such as suppliers, distributors and customers.
- Strategic decisions involve "change" in the way the business is run, including corrective actions and adjusting to different cultural issues.

Based on the above characteristics, a Strategy is the direction and scope of an organization over the long term, which achieves an advantage in the changing environment through its configuration of resources and competencies with the aim of fulfilling stakeholders' expectations.

Competitive Advantage

When an organization creates more economic value than its competitors, it is said to have achieved Competitive Advantage.

The Strategic Management Process

The Strategic Management Process is a sequential set of analyses and choices that can increase the likelihood that a company will choose a good strategy, that is, a strategy that generates competitive advantages.

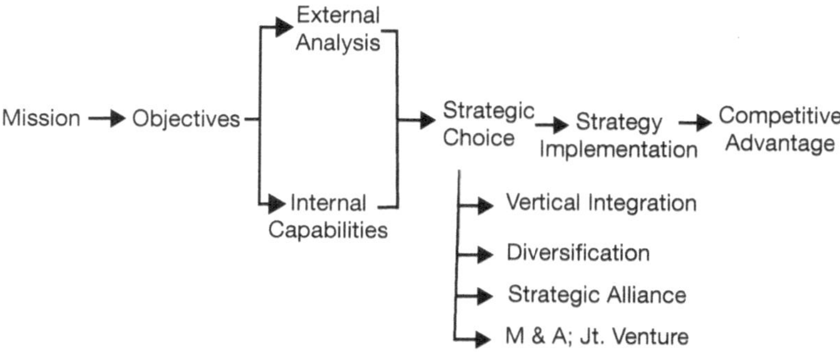

Fig. 6 Generic Strategic Process

Vision is the broad and overall ideology with which the organization is formed.

Mission is a more specific expression of the desired purpose of the organization, which ideally is in line with the values and expectations of major stakeholders, and is concerned with the scope for which the organization has come into existence. It binds the employees for the intended goal of the business.

Objectives are quantified, specific, and measurable action plan, in the line of goal setup in the mission statement.

External Analysis deals with analyzing Threats and Opportunities that exist in the marketplace in which your organization operates.

Internal Capabilities deal with the internal analysis of strengths and weaknesses that are within your own organization.

Strategic Choices are made based on the mission and the outcome of the SWOT analysis undertaken by the company. They include resources, activities, and processes for successfully conducting business activities. Strategic choices include decisions on Cost and Product related differentiations. They cover Corporate Strategies of restructuring and reorganization plan/s through Vertical Integration, Strategic Alliance, Diversification, and Mergers & Acquisitions. e

Strategy Implementation means seamless integration of Product, Service and Information flow within the organization. It includes finalizing Organization Structure, Control Processes, and Compensation Policies to suit the strategic choices made.

Competitive Advantage is a result of the successful strategic process where an organization gains sustainable core competencies over rival businesses. It ensures improved benchmark performance measured in terms of profitability, growth, and WACC (weighted average cost of capital). The business gets to a position of Competitive Advantage when it follows the said strategic process diligently and offers something unique and valuable to the marketplace.

One must note that market conditions, government policies, customer preferences, and every element in the strategic process keeps changing; hence, the strategic positioning of the company is a continuous exercise to remain competitive. Strategic positioning should have a horizon of a decade or more and not a single planning cycle. Trade-offs are essential to strategy. For example, the brand "Nirma" has a great price advantage but has quality limitations. However, Nirma still has its own target customer base for its products, which is different from the customer base of products of multinational companies.

Let us consider a case study of a company with nine decades of success to understand how the continuous process of strategic planning generates sustainable Competitive Advantage in the ever-changing market conditions.

__Walt Disney Company:__ The company was established in 1923. In 1984, the company's profit was only $242 Million (M); Theme Park operations contributed 77%, Consumer Products 22%, and Filmed Entertainment 1%; of profit. The CEO Michael Eisner was appointed in 1984 to achieve a competitive advantage for the company.

Eisner's internal and external environment assessment revealed that, "People will pay a premium price for extraordinary entertainment. We have the necessary resources to create extraordinary entertainment. Therefore, let's redeploy our resources in a different way and offer something extraordinary to people."[1]

Eisner increased admission prices at theme parks – the profit of this division increased from $186M in 1984 to $787M in 1994.

____

1   https://quizlet.com/jp/121689761/strategic-manegement-flash-cards/

He challenged animators, character developers and introduced the VHS format – profit increased from $2.42M to $ 845.00M. Lastly, he diversified into Television (ABC channel), Retail stores, Sports team, Cruise liner, Publishing, and Consumer Products – as a result, the Market Cap in 1994 increased to $28 Billion in 1994 from a meager $ 2 Billion in 1984.

EPS (earning per share) of the company increased to $1.07 in 1994 from 0.06 in 1984. However, due to disputes at the BOD level and a terrorist attack in one of the theme-parks, EPS came down to $ 0.02 in 2001. However, the company's strategic initiative of International Expansion (2005,) and acquisition of Marvel Entertainment (2009) raised EPS to $ 4.00 in 2009. The company's popular mascot Mickey Mouse merchandise sale in 2010 was over US $ 5 billion. Despite its success, the company launched a "Makeover" of the mascot to continue its popularity and kept their artists busy to develop new characters. The Company, in 2011, purchased stake of 49.56% to enter Bollywood, and at the same time entered the Chinese market with Shanghai Disney Resort to enter the expanding Asian Economies. In 2012, the company acquired UTV software communications, followed by BAMTech streaming media provider (2015), to adjust to the changing market conditions. In 2017, the company purchased 21st Century Fox, and FSN sports network to align with Disney's ESPN division. In 2018, the company undertook major Strategic Reorganization to consolidate their businesses under "Consumer Services, and Direct to consumer" distribution network. 2019 saw major acquisition of Fox Corporation (Fox Broadcasting *company, Fox television stations, Fox news channel, Fox business network, Fox Sports, and Ten Network). 2020, being Covid19 pandemic year, is not considered.*

Today Walt Disney Company has become a diversified multinational mass media and entertainment conglomerate with major subsidiaries: Pixar, Hulu, Shop-Disney, Marvel Entertainment, and MORE. 2019 Net Income is US $ 11.054 Billion, Total Assets at US $ 193.984 Billion, with 223,000 number of employees.

Mission of The Walt Disney Company:

"The mission of The Walt Disney Company is to entertain, inform, and inspire people around the globe through the power of unparallel storytelling, reflecting the iconic brands, creative minds and innovative technologies that make ours the world's premier entertainment company."[2]

To understand the gaining of perpetual competitive advantage in fierce global competition, learners are encouraged to study the synergic progress made by different successful companies by undertaking acquisitions/ disinvestments/ restructuring of their organizations and how that contributed to increased EPS/ contribution per product line.

---

2   https://thewaltdisneycompany.com/about/

In short, the strategic management process promotes mutually reinforcing linkages among activities that make the whole more than the sum of its parts.

Having considered the strategic management process, in the following chapters, we shall examine how the pragmatic Strategic Process gets defined, how a SWOT analysis is done, and how plans get implemented and executed in a company.

•••

Chapter 3

Commencement of the Strategic Process in Your Company

In this chapter, we shall be looking at the initial three stages in the process of planning and executing a business strategy to generate sustainable Competitive Advantage.

In embarking a strategic process, companies should strive for possessing the following qualities:

- <u>Envision</u>: Capability to develop a well-articulated picture of the organization to better serve the existing customers
- <u>Prepare</u>: Ability to find the shortest path between where the company is and where the company wants to get
- <u>Deliver</u>: Ability to change the organization internally to match the blueprint of the Mission and make it a world-class company.

Strategy must focus on enhancing the ability to anticipate business problems and opportunities and act preemptively. Predictive abilities allow companies to take real-time information, corelate it with historical patterns and recognize events that hold tremendous profit potential. To stay ahead of the curve, your company has to make a transition from a reactive organization to a proactive one, with a well-suited customer-centric business paradigm. This transition enables the organization to do the following:

- Anticipate customer needs and be ready to satisfy them the minute they emerge
- Be prepared for sudden events such as power shortage, spikes in demand for your products, logistic issues, or evolving customer requirements.

The Role of Top Management (Board of Directors):
Mapping the business landscape on a continuous basis is the job of the top management. The Company's Board of Directors (BOD) and CEO should regularly take stock of the company's current affairs with reference to their business and the environment in which the company operates. Brainstorming sessions at the BOD should typically address stagnation, if any, in the company's growth vis-à-vis the rate of the industry's growth; verify the intensity of competition from local and international companies; assesses the level of customer satisfaction, and review the efficiency of the company's business processes. Such periodical examination of the business purpose and its effectiveness leads to meaningful planning and execution of both short-term and long-term strategies.

The CEO must pose questions that need answering in order to establish your internal environment (strengths and weaknesses) and external environment (opportunities and threats) in your markets, your financial position, your leadership, and ultimately your organizational capabilities. The BOD should periodically assess if your CEO is capable of working as a catalyst to balance complementary and at times contradictory skills – agility to find right products and right market focus as well as the discipline to succeed – and then has the agility to refocus and adapt as the market changes.

Superior performance needs an appropriate Vision statement. The Vision is a statement of the key values that the organization is committed to and a statement of the major goals for which the organization has been incorporated. The Vision lays out some desired future state and articulates what values the company would like to promote. For example, Praj Industries Ltd. promotes values such as Integrity, Innovation, Responsibility through their Vision statement: "We aspire to be the most preferred organization for all stakeholders through environment friendly and sustainable solutions that can make the world a better place".

The Mission is crafted to provide the framework or context within which strategies are formulated; it describes what the company does and defines precise and measurable goals which the company desires to realize. For example, Premium Transmission Ltd., realizing the stagnated growth of their company (benchmarked with industry's growth), altered their Mission statement to give objective clarity to employees. The revised Mission statement read: "To be the leader in providing Mechanical Power Transmission Solutions in India with INR 10,000 million in turnover, and to have Global presence in one or more regions outside India, in five years".

Each company has unique business compulsions. Accordingly, after considering the peculiar conditions of your own business environment, your company should draw the Vision, Mission, and Objectives to provide clarity of purpose to both its employees and the world around.

We are now equipped to commence the understanding of the stage-wise strategic process. For clarity and better understanding, we shall be following a live case-study of Premier Transmission Ltd. (PTL), where the actions and achievements are supported by numbers, graphs, and results obtained.

Company background:

PTL used to be the leader in Mechanical Power Transmission Products for more than four last decades. The company has established its presence in a variety of geared product lines, viz, Worm gearbox, Helical & Bevel helical gearbox, Vertical Coal Pulverizing Mill gearbox, Planetary gearbox, Helical & Worm geared motors, Bevel Helical Cooling Tower gearbox, Fluid Coupling both Constant & variable speed, Extruder gearbox, Elevator machines, & Auto Components.

In spite of having a well-known brand, state of the art machinery, and collaborations with foreign companies, the company in the recent past has been facing various challenges. The major ones are as follows:

(i)   PTL slipped to the second position with 32% market share. Its main rival, Elecon Engineers Ltd., with 41% market share, is currently enjoying the market leadership position.

(ii)   PTL's turnover was stagnated (around INR 2500 million).

(iii) The Company's existing leadership (CEO) was not able to infuse confidence among the managerial staff.

(iv)   Lack of coordination among departments was affecting the product quality.

(v)   Business process had slowed down with a number of complaints from customers, and the company has been failing to deliver finished products on time.

The Indian market size for gearboxes and geared motors is valued over INR 20,000 million/year. Demands from OEMs and replacement-related demand from the end user industries are the sources of business for gearboxes and geared motors. The market has witnessed the entry of several multinational companies, especially from Europe. Top four Indian companies are Elecon Engineers, Premium Transmission, Shanthi Gears, and Flender (Siemens), and they account for more than 71 percent of the market share. SEW Eurodrive, Bonfiglioli, and New Allenberry Works (NAW) are other top contenders, competing to be part of the top four companies. The total gearboxes and geared motors market is forecast to grow at a CAGR of 17.3% in the next decade.

Considering PTL's own limitations and the possibility of growth, the company decided to launch an expansion plan for which both the internal and external environments needed to undergo massive changes. With this goal, the company launched an expansion plan, which is described below in 11 stages elaborated in the forthcoming chapters.

Stage 1: The CEO's initial interaction:

The newly appointed CEO called a meeting of all the Functional Heads of the company to share the Board's concerns and expectations. The discussion included a revised Mission Statement of the company and its implications and challenges for the management team. Special emphasis was also given on becoming the dominant global player in identified countries and regions.

The meeting was followed by the CEO visiting all four plants to interact with the technical staff and deliberating on the problems faced and improvements needed to enhance productivity, assessing suitability of machines with reference to customers' requirements and accordingly planning Capital Expenditure (CAPEX), assessing undercurrents hampering the team performance, and, more importantly, identifying 2nd and 3rd level executives who have the ability and spark to take on new challenges.

In the next step, the CEO had personal interactions with his key executives to know the developments gone past and to familiarize himself with the challenges faced by different departments within the organization.

The first personal interaction was scheduled with the Vice President Marketing (VPM). The discussion included the following:

- PTL losing the market share to competing companies like Elecon and Shanti, despite having the best CAGR during 2004-2009, due to a delay in providing in-time delivery of products and due to low product reliability.

- Competitor companies acquiring the latest technology and machines.
- Shanti Gears having excess installed capacity that suits special purpose/ customized gear boxes.
- Inadequate Exports.
- Lack of organic growth of sixty-five percent and balance in inorganic market.

This discussion enabled the CEO to identify the gaps and plan the strategy accordingly.

The second meeting was with the Vice President Finance (VPF). The discussion with VPF revealed the following:

- The company is enjoying adequate Working Capital facility from the consortium of banks (INR three million Fund Based and INR two million Non-fund Based) and also has a comfortable level of owned funds.
- Financial resources are sufficient to target an increased turnover as per the new Mission and new CAPEX of INR 1,000 million for the next three years.
- There is a need for five years of rolling plan with yearly budget to have a clarity for the intended action plan.

The discussion ended with the CEO asking for benchmark comparison of the margin with the immediate rival companies, Elecon and Shanti, so that while achieving the top-line target, the company should not lose out on a comfortable bottom-line/margin.

The last meeting was with the Head R&D. The discussion included the following:

- The R&D cell is separated in three sub-groups, each headed by the seniormost person. The first group looks after "Fluid Couplings" and the related; the second concentrates on "Lift machines," and the third is for "Geared Motors."
- The key activities of the R&D Cell are as follows:
    - Giving quotations for specialized/customized products or projects
    - Working on new product development
    - Giving cost estimates for both standard and specialized products
    - Mapping of process and forming groups of technical and R&D staff
    - Providing Ideal Time for completing a specialized job and comparing it with the Actual Time taken to complete the job
    - Providing guidance to technical teams as and when required, particularly for special products.

Realizing the importance of the R&D cell, the CEO wanted to know the two major concerns faced by this department. The first was not getting an adequate number of qualified engineers because the best lot preferred the Computer Industry for higher emoluments. Second, too many changes/alterations in both the "Design of product" and the "Priority of jobs" from the marketing department, due to which the work schedule got disturbed and efficiency was eroded. The allotted time for each customer order became too inadequate to produce globally acceptable product/s that included both performance and aesthetics.

Having visited and assessed the organizational issues where the "action is," the CEO comprehended many realities of the business:

- Underutilized and inadequate machines
- Lack of coordination among different departments/functions
- The need of skill upgradation for marketing engineers
- CAPEX issues despite comfortable financial position
- Need for changing key result areas (KRAs)
- Revisiting the pay scale of R&D to attract the best talent
- Repositioning the R&D setup for it to function effectively
- Finding key executives who have potential to grow for mutual benefits at the 2nd and 3rd layer of the organization.

The exercise assisted the CEO to realize where we are – where we want to reach – the challenges of change – building the future – revitalizing the team – transforming the leadership philosophy.

At this stage, we have seen how clearly the business objectives were set by the CEO after assessing the gaps in business processes. This clarity creates a platform for advancing to the second stage.

Stage 2: The Action Plan:
Armed with the Vision, Mission and clear Objectives, the CEO planned the entire process to focus on committed and concerted efforts to synergize the company's leadership team; trigger

and catalyze new thought processes; enhance and encourage team spirit; revisit the architect and reengineer the company, introspect objectively and dispassionately; evolve and implement a co-owned "action plan" that would be governed by a tangible, meaningful "time frame," channelize all organizational resources unidirectional to attain INR 10,000 million top-line in five years and be responsible and accountable "individually and collectively" to achieve this goal.

To be consistently successful, innovation has to become second nature for an engineering company like PTL. The company has to breath and live innovation, both by exploitation of existing technology (EET) and by exploitation of new technology (ENT). Innovation does not mean only product improvement; innovation encompasses Transactions, Processes & Paradigms.

In consideration of the second line of command being highly qualified, experienced and mildly rigid, the CEO decided to form a "Core Team" to ease acceptance and ensure effective implementation of the strategic plan to be shaped. The said Methodology greatly assisted the organization in focusing on becoming a world–class organization, which works effectively on two curves at the same time – the first being "present operational improvements," and the second being "represent future innovations." Innovations include products, processes, and mind-set of employees. Simultaneously, such organizations reduce the chances of human fallibility when the Core Team of the company executives, as a group, is trained to initiate and to drive The Change.

The outcome of stage two can be depicted as follows:

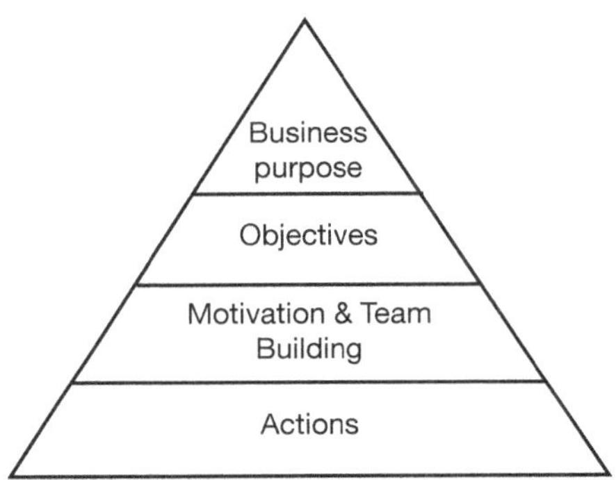

Fig. 7 The Pyramid of Goals and Action Plan

The "strategic initiative" was code named "STAR" to provide the select Core Team with a unique identity and recognition. The acronym stands for Strategic Transformation for Achieving desired Results. This Core Team in reality would act as the "catalyst of change."

•••

Chapter 4
Developing a Winning Team

A winning team is a motivated lot that is capable of defining, shaping, and implementing a Strategic Process that creates a sustainable competitive advantage. Such a team enables companies to promote innovations and creativity, increase the relevance of the firm's actions to attract customers, improve productivity, introduce lean business processes, attract good brains, and ultimately, increase returns to the stakeholders.

A Case in Point – The Taj Group

We are aware of the courageous behavior of the Taj Group employees when their hotel was under a terrorist attack. To inculcate a culture of motivation and create a winning team, in 2001, Taj had launched a loyalty program called STARS (Special Thanking and Recognition System). The initiative was designed to inspire employees to go beyond their routine tasks and responsibilities while also enjoying their work, and for such an initiative, Taj was awarded the prestigious international "Hermes Award."

Taj was again ranked the best in the "World's Finest Luxury Grand Palaces" category at the esteemed 101 Executive Summit held in Germany in the year 2023.[3]

Like Taj, all progressive companies engage employees to be fully motivated and try to instill "Core Values" in them.

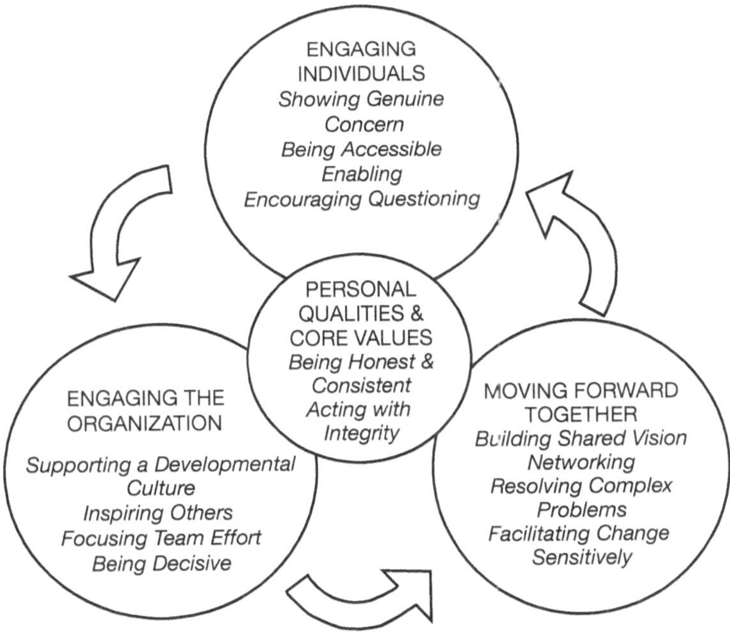

Fig. 8 Core Values

3   https://www.ihcltata.com/press-room/taj-wins-the-worlds-finest-luxury-grand-palaces-award-at-the-101-best-executive-summit-in-germany/#:~:text=MUMBAI%2C%20DECEMBER%205%2C%202023%3A,-Finest%20Luxury%20Grand%20Palaces'%20category.

Let us now proceed with the understanding of what your company can do to get similar results and how to go about creating your own Winning Team.

Stage 3: Formation of a Core Team

At PTL, getting down to where the action is and asking relevant questions made the CEO understand the realities of the business and enabled him to establish personal connections; he realized the options that were different from his earlier thought process. The CEO's initial interaction with the staff at all plants and offices enabled him to select executives from the 2nd and 3rd line of command, along with Functional Heads, for the composition of the Core Team. Accordingly, a Core Team consisting of fourteen executives representing cross-functional areas of business was formed. Selected juniors or future leaders from line and staff functions were eventually expected to fit into the role of "succession planning" as well.

The Team was given a specific timeframe of 6 to 8 months for finding pragmatic solutions for the challenges faced by the organization. Bi-monthly "Review and Coordination" meetings were scheduled, under the chairmanship of the CEO. Rightfully, the Team was given the requisite freedom and authority to seek suitable information from various departments and factories that were located at different places. The Team was even given authority to appoint an independent agency to assess industry and market growth since it was clear that PTL had to create a "Blue Ocean" in addition to being competitive in the "Red Ocean," both in India and the global market. Blue Ocean strategy is the simultaneous pursuit of differentiation and low cost to open up a new marketplace, thereby making the competition irrelevant. Red Ocean is the known marketplace, where industry boundaries are defined and companies try to outperform their rivals to grab a greater share of the existing market.

The intended change was planned through practical and applied management techniques, reliance on threadbare discussions and deliberations, and exchange of views along with constructive dialogue. The ideology for the functioning of the core team was, "Let us generate Light, not Heat."

With this, the core team was set to drive the strategic agenda, implement the change process, create a continuous improvement in the mindset throughout the organization, and maintain a disciplined and accountable approach to growth.

Agenda for improvement

The agenda entrusted to the Core Team was as follows:

(a)   Identify, analyze, and suggest solutions to overcome the current inefficiencies in products as well as processes.

(b)   Commence the thought process on how to promote innovative products.

(c)   Chart a "Roadmap" for the next five years so that the company achieves its newly crafted mission of reaching a targeted turnover of INR 10,000 million and becoming a global player in some parts of the world. The team was asked to formulate a strategy for long-term and sustainable advantage to the organization and not to restrict themselves to short-lived corrections.

The CEO was aware that business is complex, and so is the team's thinking, which adds to the existing complexities and so on in a seemingly endless cycle. Therefore, it was important to keep the "Strategic Agenda" and its "Process" simple and pragmatic. The "exercise of change" had to be inculcated in employees' day-to-day functioning and with a very small deviation from their daily work routine. A simple and pragmatic process was chosen to find long-term solutions to improve productivity and develop a permanent habit in all concerned. Simple language and concepts can promote an action-oriented dialogue across the organization. It is a known fact that in order to make something simple, one has to know the subject very well, and a simple process is more likely to lead to action. Ironically, simple philosophies, ideas, and practices are unlikely to be imitated by competitor companies.

Accordingly, the Core Team was asked to meet on alternate Saturdays (after office hours) to work on the strategic intent of the company under the guidance of the CEO. This approach enabled working on long-term solutions without disturbing the day-to-day business exigencies.

Stage 4: Assimilation of the Core Team

The chosen team had a combination of young, talented, and knowledgeable juniors, along with functional heads and seniors. These fresh faces, second and third-level managers and supervisors, were not exposed to the "meeting culture." Making them participate freely in brainstorming sessions, where their views could be different from their seniors, was not an easy task. At the same time, it was necessary for fresh ideologies to come forward for discussion, debate, and improvement. This in turn was expected to automatically develop the second and third line of command to take mature decisions and serve in the succession plan of the company. Such junior executives are not very occupied, unlike big honchos, and pay attention to the important details, stay connected with important improvements, and stay close as a team. They are never too high and mighty to listen and learn, to be curious and inquisitive and open to new ideas.

To bring in a cohesive culture among seniors and juniors and to bond them as a unified team, the CEO planned a deliberation on some caselets. These cases pertained to multinational companies handling their own critical situations along with the strategies successfully deployed by them. The situations chosen in the said corporate insights were such that they were relevant and comparable to the problems faced by PTL. The team was broken into smaller groups, each group having a combination of seniors and juniors. Care was also taken to form cross-functional groups. Each group was required to study the situation given in the caselet and discuss it among themselves. One of the group members was asked to present the strategies adopted by the multinational, and his counterpart from the same group was asked to present the group's view on a comparable situation in PTL.

The first corporate case was that of *Mahindra and Mahindra (M&M)*, covering a "Backward integration to achieve competitive advantage."[4] PTL related issues arose about having their own foundry (backward integration), in-house machining jobs (replacing lower quality due to outsourcing), and the possibility of electric motor manufacturing (diversification).

The next case was *Cadbury India*, covering "Cadbury's strategies to be a market leader."[5] From PTL's perspective, the following topics came up during the discussion: Concentrate on core-competencies in a select product range of Worm, Helical, Geared Motors, and Fluid Couplings; develop and launch new products every year; revisit "make or buy" (outsourcing) policies; establish a strong service network; discontinue the non-performing products; and improvise on the dealers' feedback and on market surveys.

The third case was "Intensity of competition between *Proctor and Gamble vis-à-vis Hindustan Lever (P&G v/s HLL)*."[6] From PTL's point-of-view, these topics came up: To match the intense competition from the rivals (Elecon and Shanthi

---

4   Corporate Insight M&M Backward Integration to achieve Competitive Advantage
5   Corporate Insight Cadbury's Strategies of a Market Leader
6   Corporate Insight Intensity of Competition

Gears), PTL had to become cost-effective; discounts should be extended to customers instead of dealers, and there should be intensification of the direct distribution network.

The fourth corporate insight was from *Dabur India Ltd. (DIL)*, on "Product modification to suit customer requirements."[7] PTL perspectives that came up for discussion: Branding of Universal Modular Gear Boxes required to improve power-to-weight ratio, improve packaging, and bring consistency in product quality.

The last corporate insight was from *Tanishq*, (a TATA enterprise): "Differentiation is the key to marketing success."[8] The team realized that though the differentiation for Tanishq came from marketing, in the case of PTL, it would come from technology. Taking a clue from the Tanishq situation, the Core Team realized that PTL needed to work on improvement in the technical reliability of the products to win customers' trust, which demands improving design specifications, bringing innovative and compact designs, better craftsmanship, better material quality, the final product strictly meeting the performance parameters, and lastly, such a technically proven product must be offered at the right pricing.

---

7   Corporate Insight Dabur India Ltd. (DIL) Product modification to suit customer requirements

8   Corporate Insight Tanishq - Differentiation is the key to marketing success

The "Corporate Insights" from the said cases achieved many desired results. First of all, many of PTL's burning issues came on a platter automatically. Secondly, the technically sound young executives who were not exposed to the "meeting culture" got the required courage to put up their valuable suggestions despite opposition from seniors. Thirdly, since the issues pertained to multinationals, free and frank discussions took place on alternative strategies and this wisdom could be judiciously used in the working of PTL. Fourthly, everybody got a chance to iron out their presentation skills. Lastly, the team was bound together as one force.

Stage 5: Addressing "Pain Areas"

The stagnation of a company accumulates grievances. The CEO wanted to honestly address them at this stage and develop mature and open leadership at all levels of the organization. The Core Team was told that there were many challenges to change the way they were doing business. While some felt "training and technical knowledge" was needed, others may have thought of improving the "Process Planning Management." Some opined that the "Paint Booth" be shifted near the completion area, while some felt the interdepartmental communication needed to be improved, and so on. However, consensus had to be developed, and for that, he challenged all the members of the Core Team to develop a free and frank issue-based opinion based on each member's "wish list." Accordingly, a questionnaire was given to all the participants to individually respond to each question. The response was expected to reveal what they felt as an individual and how they perceived the company's current standing and future growth. To avoid any prejudice, personal details were avoided in the response sheet.

One of the questions was, "Do you wish to enhance your learning?" and all the 14 members responded with "Yes."

To the question, "How much do you contribute to the company's performance?" 11 felt "A lot," one felt "Insignificant" and one was "Not sure."

However, the immediate question was, "Do you think you can contribute more?" and the thumping positive response from all the 14 was "Yes."

As to the question, "How is the teamwork in the company?" none of them opted for "Excellent" and 10 felt it "Can improve" but only 4 felt it "Should improve."

As regards the organization's perspective, one of the questions was "How do you rate the competition in the industry?" To this, 12 opined "Strong and competent" whereas only 2 chose the option "hardly strong."

To the question, "How do you rate your own team?" 6 chose "Strong and competent," whereas, 8 felt it was "Complacent."

The next very pertinent question was, "Do you wish PTL to become a world-class company?" A majority, i.e., 12 opted for "Yes," 1 felt "It's tough," and 1 chose "We should not attempt."

To the last tricky question as to "What should we change to become world class?" a thumping majority of 11 opted for "Mindset," though other options were equally likely and tempting, such as "Direction, coordination, and team spirit."

The overall response to the questionnaire was positive. The team reaffirmed that given suitable guidance and with a cohesive culture, the team was capable of turning the corner.

The consolidated response sheet from the Core Team of 14 executives to the questionnaire is produced below for in-depth understanding.

Table 1: Part 1 Assessment of Employees' Personal Responses

Stage 07 : Addressing Pain Areas

YOU

Question No. 1	A	How do you describe yourself ?	An excellent professional	3
	B		A good professional	11
	C		OK professional	0
Question No. 2	A	Do you wish to enhance your learning?	Yes	14
	B		No	0
Question No. 3	A	How much do you contribute to PTL's Performance?	A Lot	11
	B		Insignificant	1
	C		Not Sure	1
Question No. 4	A	Do you think you can contribute more?	Yes	14
	B		No	0

Question No. 5	A	How do you think you can contribute more?	If we change the structure	0
	B		If we change the systems	4
	C		If 1 change myself	11
Question No. 6	A	What are you?	A Manager	2
	B		A Leader	12
Question No. 7	A	Are you involved in strategic planning?	Yes	11
	B		No	3
Question No. 8	A	The Teamwork in PTL	Excellent	0
	B		Can Improve	10
	C		Should Improve	4
Question No. 9	A	Are you satisfied with your own performance?	100%	1
	B		75%	12
	C		50%	1
Question No. 10	A	Are you satisfied with your peers' performance?	100%	0
	B		75%	8
	C		50%	6
Question No. 11	A	According to you, a good professional should...	Follow the systems	1
	B		Maintain the systems	0
	C		Challenge the status quo	13

Table 2: Part 2 Assessment of the Company's Standing

PTL

Question No. 1	A	Premium is a --	World Class Company	1
	B		OK Company	13
Question No. 2	A	Our Product Quality is -	Excellent	0
	B		Good	7
	C		Ok	7
Question No. 3	A	Our Customers are -	100% satisfied	0
	B		80% satisfied	12
	C		Not satisfied	2
Question No. 4	A	Our Cost & Prices are -	Competitive	9
	B		Not Competitive	5
Question No. 5	A	In the Market,	We follow the competition	11
	B		We proactively lead	3
Question No. 6a	A	How is the working environment?	Challenging	7
	B		Comfortable	4
Question No. 6b	A		Transparent	6
	B		Opaque	7
Question No. 6c	A		Merit based	5
	B		Subjective	8
Question No. 6d	A		Conservative	11
	B		Dynamic	1
Question No. 6e	A		Clarity about accountability	4
	B		Ambiguity & Vagueness	8
Question No. 7	A	How do you rate Competition?	Strong & competent	12
	B		So so	2
Question No. 8	A	How do you rate your own Team?	Strong & competent	6
	B		Complacent	8

Question No. 9	A	Do you wish to become a World Class Company?	Yes	12
	B		It's Tough	1
	C		We should not attempt	1
Question No. 10	A	What should we change to become World Class?	Mindset	11
	B		Direction	2
	C		Coordination	1
	D		Teamwork	7
	E		Systems	5
	F		Technology	6

This brainstorming session gave a new dimension to the team. It reaffirmed their positive outlook to the ongoing "ConsultMent" process, and the team opened up for self-improvement.

Stage 6: A Unified Team with a Common Goal

Richard Pascale has said, "A butterfly is no more caterpillar or a better or improved caterpillar, a butterfly is a different creature."

The Core Team with a "Common Goal" truly evolved through the last five stages of development. Having discussed and debated on a variety of business issues and finding a solution acceptable by all departments, the entire Core Team, with their positive attitude, became a team that could freely and frankly debate with their counterparts on any aspect of common interest. To a great extent, each member could now perceive their colleague's point of view. Airing out the "pain areas" along with discussions on some of the multinational company's issues and strategies gave them the required comfort to freely operate within the group. A win-win solution from each department's point of view became a reality in conducting the business. At the same time, evolution through the stated stages along with the ability of the new leadership/ CEO gave them confidence and comfort.

Creative but simple steps taken so far led the foundation to collectively march toward PTL's mission. As per the findings of the research published by IBM, based on the worldwide research with over 1500 CEO's and executives, creativity was identified as the most important leadership competency for enterprises seeking competitive advantage in the contemporary business world. Similarly, fostering creativity at PTL meant recognition of two different dimensions: "The Individual" and "The Collective."

Firstly, at an individual level, the leaders and the employees at PTL understood their own creative potential. Truly exploring personal creativity can reveal hidden treasures and open the door to a more grounded creative culture. Secondly, collective creativity was determined by the way PTL employees interacted in order to find new solutions to innovate and solve problems. Both dimensions of creativity are not only tightly connected but also intertwined in the way that one kind of creativity needs the other to fully harvest its potential.

At PTL, the Core Team became a different creature and each member of the team was positively charged to take on the company's mission with full confidence and promise. The target of achieving the sales turnover of INR 10000 million turned from impossible to possible, and regaining the Competitive Advantage over rival companies became the Common Goal. The CEO and BOD at this stage became confident that the revitalized Core Team was now fully prepared to take on business challenges as a unified group.

•••

Chapter 5

Executing a Strategic Plan

Having commenced the strategic process and after developing a winning team, PTL proceeded with drafting a strategic plan starting with analyzing internal and external environments.

Stage 7: SWORT Analysis

Facilitating an open discussion to address grievances and pain points, the integrated Core Team successfully alleviated historical tensions and complaints. This transformation fostered a motivated and objective group, poised to impartially examine the challenges encountered by the company. To initiate the process, the Core Team pragmatically engaged in a SWORT (Strengths, Weaknesses, Opportunities, Risk Identification, and Threats) analysis, incorporating risk elements and probability assessments to quantify pertinent considerations.

The Core Team meticulously examined internal strengths and weaknesses, while simultaneously scrutinizing external opportunities and threats, aligning with the strategic approach typically undertaken by CEOs. This thorough analysis uncovered various areas for potential improvement, exemplified as follows:

1. **Strengths (Internal):** Streamlined communication channels and a cohesive leadership structure.

   PTL's Action Plan: Leverage strong communication channels for efficient decision-making and reinforce leadership cohesion.

   The outcome of the exercise threw open the following Strengths at PTL:

   - 40 + years of experience in manufacturing industrial gearboxes and fluid couplings.
   - A strong, well-known brand.
   - Market leader in Worm gearboxes.
   - All mechanical power transmissions under one roof (Worm/ Helical / Planetary gearboxes, Fluid Couplings, etc.).
   - Top management's support for R&D focus. For example: Load test facility up to 500 hp.

2. **Weaknesses (Internal):** Reliance on outdated technology, infrastructure, and a need for skill development.

   PTL's Action Plan: Invest in technology upgrades to enhance operational efficiency and implement training programs to address skill gaps.

   The outcome of the exercise threw open the following Weaknesses at PTL:

   - Many obsolete product designs with lower power-to-weight ratios
   - Long process time and delays in delivery schedules

- Non-consistent quality of products (many times due to outsourced material such as Castings)
- Remuneration not in line with the best in the market
- Weak vendor base

3. **Opportunities (External):** Emerging markets and potential strategic partnerships.

   PTL's Action Plan: Explore entry into untapped markets and form strategic partnerships to expand the company's reach.

   The outcome of the exercise threw open the following Opportunities at PTL:

   - Spread of plants at four different locations (merger of a couple of units/disinvestment in one of the plants/ Trade Union issues of bargainable staff's voluntary retirement and/or golden handshake identified for further discussion)
   - Possibility of backward integration and starting own foundry
   - Management's willingness for new technical collaboration or acquisitions, if the right fit and right price are available
   - Possibility of a common store in the central part of India to achieve lower inventory, savings in storage cost, faster delivery of finished goods to customers, centralized bulk procurement, savings in overheads, etc.

4. **Threats (External):** Increasing competition and potential regulatory changes.

   PTL's Action Plan: Conduct market research to identify unique selling points and stay informed about regulatory shifts to adapt proactively.

   The outcome of the exercise threw open the following Threats at PTL:

- The possibility of large international companies setting up their own production facilities in India, affecting the company's local market share
- A wide product range and their numerous inventory items posing problems in establishing effective SAP implementation
- Inventory pile up with slow/ non-moving items blocking the working capital and in turn increasing the cost of finished goods

In addition to SWOT, the following risk factors were identified for specific deliberations and suitable action.

5. **PTL-specific Risk Identification**

- Backward integration in the foundry being labor-intensive (bargainable workforce)
- Duplication of support staff and line staff due to four different locations
- Difficulty in attracting young engineers for the manufacturing activity
- Direct production of new product/s without waiting for prototype, along with inconsistency in quality

Based on the SWORT analysis, the Core Team decided to brainstorm on different products manufactured by the company and work out the BCG Matrix[9] for their major product lines. BCG matrix, an analytical tool in business strategy, helps corporates to analyze their business units or product lines and helps the

---

9   The concept of BCG Matrix was first applied by Bruce Henderson, Boston Consulting Group, 1970.

company to allocate resources. This growth-share matrix also analyzes each product's relative market share and growth rate to plan fresh investments and disinvestment strategies.

The resultant matrix for PTL products worked out as follows.

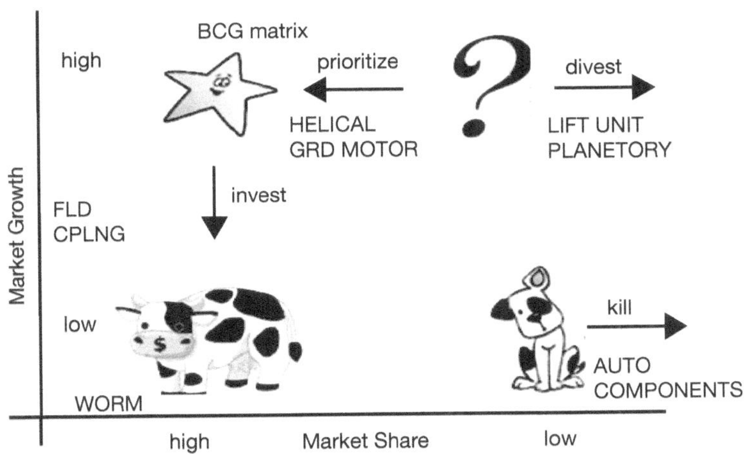

Fig. 9 BCG Matrix for PTL Products

(Source: PTL's internal record)

Worm gearbox was identified as having a high share in the market with low growth prospects. It was decided to keep this product in the current portfolio for the time being as a cash cow.

Helical gears was in a high-growth market and here, the company's share was relatively high in the market. This product group was generating a high-income margin. It was suggested to build on this product group, which could be grouped under "Stars."

Auto components had a low market growth and the company's share was also low due to cutthroat competition. These products contributed less and consumed a larger part of input resources. The team suggested keeping a low profile in this product line or disinvesting gradually in them. These were a canine version of real turkeys and were grouped under "Dogs."

Lift Unit and Planetary gears had a high market growth but the company's share had been low. Such products absorbed a lot of money/resources when the company tried to increase the market share. It was decided to probe into the relevant details and study the scope before the company went in for expansion, and these could be grouped under "Question Marks."

The final outcome of the BCG Matrix was supported by an independent Market Survey conducted by Frost & Sullivan. As per their study, Helical GRD Motors, with high market growth and high market share, remains a star performing product. Planetary Gearbox was in growth stage of the product cycle; Auto Components was in severe competition from firms that specialised only in this product, and Worm Gearbox was in between the maturity and decline stages of the product cycle.

***Stage 8*: Strategic Organizational Restructuring**

As we advanced to Stage 8, the culmination of our transformative journey, it became evident that the knowledge acquired in the preceding stages necessitated a profound restructuring of our organization to attain our desired objectives. The old organizational structure was as follows:

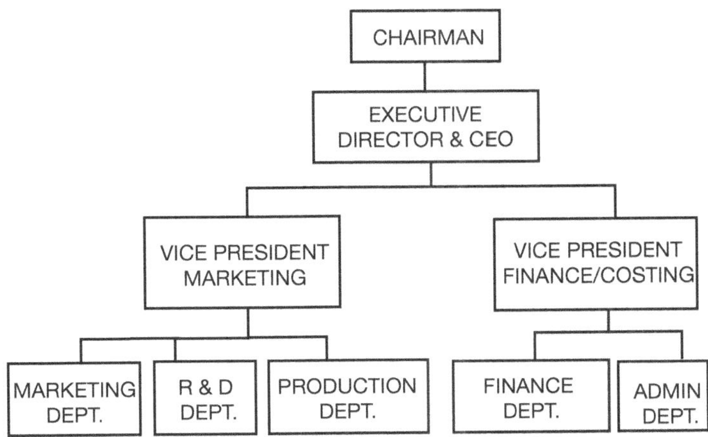

Fig. 10 Old Organizational Chart

(Source: PTL's internal record)

In hindsight, our previous organizational structure proved insufficient. The Team recognized that the crux of our ascent to a leadership position lay in Technical Innovations and the implementation of efficient Business Processes. Thus, a strategic realignment was imperative, granting due importance and autonomy to R&D and Production functions.

Simultaneously, Marketing was directed to concentrate on Key Result Areas (KRAs), seizing the expanded market space and enhancing customer satisfaction. The circumstances called for a strategic shift in our organizational structure.

In line with this strategic vision, the head of R&D, which is a pivotal staff function, was elevated to the esteemed level of Vice President, aligning with other functional heads. Additionally, the crucial Technology/Production function now fell directly under the vigilant supervision of the CEO.

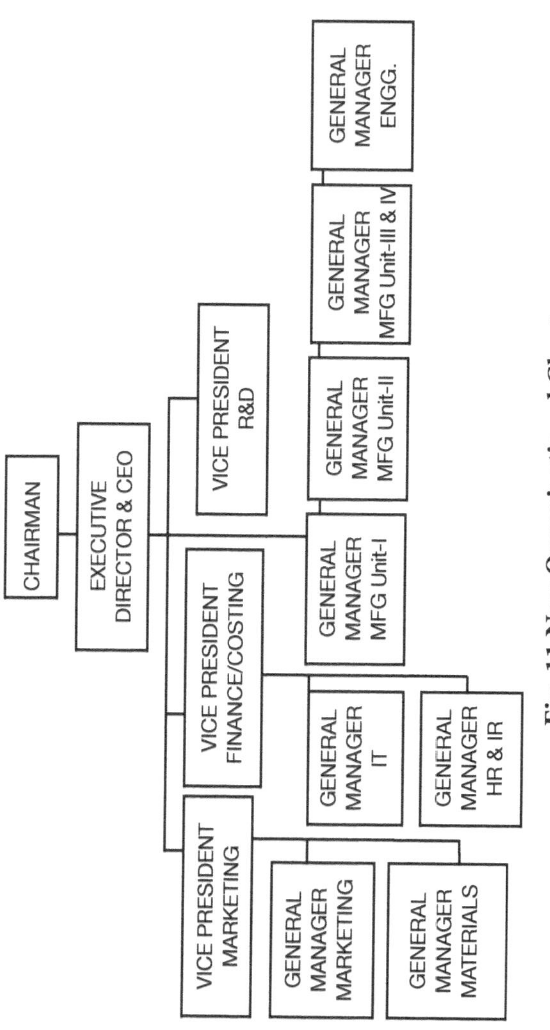

Fig. 11 New Organizational Chart

(Source: Outcome of the ConsultMent Process at PTL)

In conjunction with these organizational changes, a meticulously revised chart signified the management's unwavering commitment to engineering innovations, superior product design, and ongoing business process enhancements.

This refined organizational framework, bolstered by the enhanced KRAs, stood as a testament to our unwavering pursuit of strategic excellence and the fortification of our leadership position in the industry.

Stage 9: Strategic Future Readiness

In the relentless pursuit of success in the contemporary business landscape, organizations must empower their workforce, prioritize customer focus, instill personal accountability, and foster goal-oriented entrepreneurship. To assert control in their respective industries and shape markets for tomorrow, companies must evolve new breakthrough strategies. This evolution demands a paradigm shift in corporate strategy thinking, encompassing the mobilization of employees around "strategic intent," resource leveraging across organizational boundaries, identification and exploitation of "white space" opportunities, core competency redeployment, consistent customer amazement, exploration of new competitive spaces in marketing, and building of brand value.

While the earlier stages and SWOT analysis provided a clear direction for the Core Team, it became evident that this alone was insufficient to achieve our targeted mission. A departure from routine thinking was imperative. The Core Team needed to assess whether PTL is genuinely future-ready and possesses the capability to shape its intended future and regenerate success in the years to come.

To gauge this readiness, a set of assumptions was presented to the Core Team, prompting them to evaluate PTL against competitors on key parameters through the following structured questionnaire.

What does the Core Team think about the future preparedness of PTL against that of competitors' preparedness?

Conventional and Reactive	.	.	.	.	.	Distinctive and Far-sighted

Which issue is absorbing more of the senior managers' attention?

Reengineering Core Processes	.	.	.	.	.	Regenerating Core Strategies

Within the industry, do competitors view our company as more of a rule-taker or a rule-maker?

Mostly a Rule-taker	.	.	.	.	.	Mostly a Rule-maker

What are we better at, improving operational efficiency or creating fundamentally new businesses?

Operational Efficiency	.	.	.	.	.	New Business Development

What percentage of our advantage-building efforts focus on catching up with competitors versus building advantages new to the industry?

Mostly Catching up with Others	.	.	.	.	.	Mostly New to the Industry

To what extent has our transformation agenda been set by competitors' action versus being set by our own unique vision of the future?

Largely Driven by Competitors	.	.	.	.	.	Largely Driven by Our Vision

To what extent am I as a senior manager, an engineer working on the present, or an architect designing the future?

Mostly an Engineer	.	.	.	.	.	Mostly an Architect

Among employees, what is the balance between anxiety and hope?

Mostly Anxiety	.	.	.	.	.	Mostly Hope

Fig. 12 Questionnaire

(Source: Gary Hamel and C. K. Prahalad, "Competing for the Future."

Published by Harvard Business School Press, 1998.)

The responses revealed a tendency of PTL to expend excessive energy preserving the past rather than adequately focusing on shaping the future.

This introspective exercise facilitated a profound understanding within the Core Team of the mindset required to become "Future Ready." The exhaustive brainstorming sessions unveiled a realization that PTL was far from embodying a "Future Ready" mentality. The group emerged from the deliberations with a newfound clarity, understanding the need to transcend the confines of a "percent incremental improvements" mindset. Instead of dwelling on preserving the past, the realization dawned that directing energy and resources toward future developments is the key to strategic success.

Stage 10: Strategic Focus Areas & Benchmarking
Focus areas

In pursuit of strategic excellence, Stage 10 marked a pivotal moment for PTL as the enthusiastic Core Team underwent a structured subdivision into four sub-teams: Leader Team, Innovator Team, Visionary Team, and Excellence Team. Each team, led by a designated team leader and comprising Champions, embraced a cross-functional character, mirroring the diversity of the Core Team. This strategic move aimed to infuse positivity and enthusiasm throughout the organization by involving additional employees in the process.

To guide their efforts, participants were challenged by the CEO to think differently and address fundamental questions such as these: How are we contributing to our customers' prosperity? What is the quality of our people in shaping a unique value proposition for our customers? How effectively is our pricing aligned with attributes our customers highly value?

The resulting "Focus Areas" were meticulously identified, each team taking ownership of critical aspects with a clear mandate to identify limitations, deliberate on possible options, and act decisively to drive improvements.

1. **Design & Development Excellence**
   - Increase Lift Units sales to 100 units from the current 40-45.
   - Achieve INR 10 million sales of SM & BM Geared Motors from the existing INR 5 million.
   - Reduce manufacturing cost of the Helical Gear series by 30%.
   - Reduce manufacturing cost of PSV Coupling by 35%.

2. **Excellence in Marketing**
   - Increase sales of Extruder Gear Boxes by 100%.
   - Increase sales of Fluid Couplings by 50%.
   - Increase sales of Planetary Gear Boxes to INR 270 million.
   - Address lacunae identified in earlier discussions on the department's functioning.

3. **Excellence in Manufacturing**
   - Enhance Assembly Capacity to INR 100 million per month for Helical Gear Boxes in the Pune unit.
   - Increase Casting Capacity to cater to a business of INR 6,000 million per year across all units.
   - Improve Aesthetics and Packing for the full range of products.
   - Prioritize improvement in Worm and Helical Gear Boxes due to their substantial contribution to profitability.

4.   Transactional Excellence/Business Process Excellence

- Reduce time by 75% in Manual SOF (special order finalization) to release BOM (bill of material) for non-standard Gear Boxes.
- Collect old C Forms within 4 months and C Forms for current orders within 6 months from the completion of the financial year.
- Ensure on-time payment to suppliers and reduce purchase costs by 10%.
- Achieve on-time delivery of Outsourced Material & Castings.

Each Sub-Team diligently presented their findings, solutions, and recommendations to the Core Committee, aligning their plans with customer needs. These proposals were subsequently presented to the CEO for approval and seamless incorporation into the organizational system.

Benchmarking

Benchmarking is a process for improving performance by constantly identifying, understanding, and adapting best practices and processes followed inside and outside the company and implementing the results. The main emphasis of benchmarking is on improving the given business operation or process by exploiting the best practices, and not the best performance. A typical benchmarking exercise is a four-stage process, involving planning, data collection, data analysis, and reporting and adaptation.

The typical benchmarking process was done at Xerox Plc as follows.

Fig. 13 Professor Johnson's Concept of Benchmarking

(Source: Xerox Plc.)

In 2004, Dabur Ltd. undertook the benchmarking process against the rival FMCGs, viz. Nestle, Colgate-Palmolive, and P&G, highlighting the following:

- Dabur's P/E (price-to-earnings) ratio was less than 24; for others it was more than 40.
- Dabur's NWC (net working capital) was Rs. 2.2 billion; others were managing their business in less than half of that amount.
- Dabur's OPM (operating profit margin) was at 12%, whereas Colgate & Nestle at 16% & P&G at 18% were much better.

PTL conducted a meticulous benchmarking exercise against competitors with a similar product range, focusing on the Operating Margin. The findings were as follows:

Table 3: Comparative Profitability Statement

PTL vis-a-vis major competitors, for the base year

Premium Energy Transmission Ltd		Shanthi Gears Ltd		Elecon Engineering Co. Ltd	
Particulars	**%**	**Particulars**	**%**	**Particulars**	**%**
Gross Sales		Gross Sales		Gross Sales	
Excise duty		Excise duty		Excise duty	
Net Sales		**Net Sales**		**Net Sales**	
Other Income	*	other Income	*	other Income	*
Net Revenue	**100%**	**Net Revenue**	**100%**	**Net Revenue**	**100%**
Raw Material	49.5%	Raw Material	30.2%	Raw Material	67.6%
Employee Cost	10.7%	Employee Cost	13.0%	Employee Cost	4.6%
Other Mfg. Expenses	12.8%	Other Mfg. Expenses	0.0%	Other Mfg. Expenses	0.0%
Selling & admin. Expenses	7.7%	Selling & admin. Expenses	14.2%	Selling & admin. Expenses	11.5%
Miscellaneous Expenses	0.0%	Miscellaneous Expenses	0.0%	Miscellaneous Expenses	0.0%
Total expenditure	**80.7%**	**Total expenditure**	**57.4%**	**Total expenditure**	**83.7%**
EBIDTA	19.3%	EBIDTA	42.6%	EBIDTA	16.3%
Interest	2.5%	Interest	2.0%	Interest	5.4%
Depreciation	3.9%	Depreciation	22.1%	Depreciation	3.2%
Profit Before Tax	12.9%	Profit Before Tax	18.5%	Profit Before Tax	7.7%
Tax Provision	4.7%	Tax Provision	6.5%	Tax Provision	2.3%
Profit After Tax	8.2%	Profit After Tax	12.0%	Profit After Tax	5.4%

*Comparative figures not available

(Source: PTL Internal Records)

(EBIDTA as a percentage of sales indicates the efficiency with which the production activity is carried out. Lower wastage and rework result in higher earnings before interest, depreciation, tax, and amortization. Interest indicates how efficiently the funds are managed by keeping the working capital cycle at a minimum. PTL's selling and administration expenses indicate that probably marketing should be done more aggressively, and many more relevant indications were obtained for taking corrective actions.)

Moreover, benchmarking was extended to study the GDP growth vis-à-vis the Gearbox industry growth, offering a macro perspective on industry dynamics. This comprehensive analysis revealed both the company's YOY growth and the challenges posed by the increased competition from multinational players in the Indian market.

Table 4: India's GDP Growth vis-à-vis Gearbox Industry Growth

Year	Previous Year 6 (N-6) (in Cr.)	Previous Year 5 (N-5) (in Cr.)	Previous Year 4 (N-4) (in Cr.)	Previous Year 3 (N-3) (in Cr.)	Previous Year 2 (N-2) (in Cr.)	Previous Year 1 (N-1) (in Cr.)	Base Year (N) (in Cr.)	CAGR
PTL	89.00	156.00	208.00	261.00	273.00	301.00	361.00	26.3%
Shanthi	121.00	162.00	201.00	244.00	253.00	122.00	163.00	5.1%
Elecon	215.00	245.00	318.00	389.00	394.00	424.00	519.00	15.8%
NAW	39.00	48.00	58.00	68.00	22.00	95.00	110.00	18.9%
Flender	68.00	85.00	103.00	122.00	81.00	170.00	200.00	19.7%
	532.00	**696.00**	**888.00**	**1084.00**	**1023.00**	**1112.00**	**1353.00**	**16.8%**

	N-6	N-5	N-4	N-3	N-2	N-1	Base	CAGR
GDP Growth Rate (%) at factor cost			9.48	9.57	9.32	6.72	8.39	8.39
IIP (for Mfg in terms of % growth with base year = 2004-05)			10.30%	15.00%	18.40%	2.50%	4.80%	9.00%
Manufacturing Growth (Rs. Billion)		4990.2	5704.58	6290.72	6563.02	7197.29	7742	**7.6%***

*CAGR

(Source: PTL Internal Records)

GDP and IIP (for manufacturing) have been, in the recent past, growing at around 8% to 9%. PTL's average CAGR, which measures year on year growth rate of a company based on the actuals of the last 7 years, has been satisfactory at 26.3%, in comparison to major players in the gearbox industry. However, increasing competition from multinationals in the Indian market along with the current stagnation at PTL were major concerns and urgently needed some strategic initiative.

The insights gained through benchmarking and the study of the YOY company's growth with IIP provided the Core Team with a nuanced understanding of PTL's standing vis-à-vis the main competitors. Areas such as efficiency in production activities, management of funds, marketing aggressiveness, and other relevant aspects were revealed. This exercise prompted strategic initiatives, ensuring PTL's competitiveness in the dynamic market environment.

In response to these findings, strategic initiatives were implemented, including enhancing productivity, inventory optimization, and cost reduction measures. The emphasis on lean business processes aimed to save both costs and time, fostering a culture of continuous improvement and ensuring PTL's agility in a rapidly evolving industry landscape.

Based on the benchmarking and comparison of IIP growth vis-à-vis company-wise YOY growth, the following specific actionable points came to light.

1. Updated information on pending C forms (Sales Tax adjustment mechanism), which have financial implications, was generated, and based on this data, the marketing

department was given a time-bound schedule to recover the pending forms.

2. To avoid the recurrence of pending C Forms (currently replaced by GST), a task force of three employees representing Finance, Purchase, and Sales departments was formed to continuously monitor and maintain the updated status.

3. For the problem of inventory pile-up with slow/ non-moving items, which chokes the working capital flow, a separate task force of three members representing Finance, Stores, and Procurement departments was appointed. The task force found that four plants put together had INR 8 million worth of stocks as slow-moving and INR 12 million worth in the category of non-moving.

4. A policy decision was made to disinvest from non-moving stocks. It was noticed that the delay in payment to creditors led to cost escalation by suppliers. The Core Team decided to centralize the A category items needed by all the plants and to renegotiate the prices with the suppliers based on on-time payments.

5. The Finance team was asked to study the cost-plus-percentage-of-cost (CPPC) methodology to be offered to select vendors of semi-finished products, which was expected to reduce costs considerably. This methodology would assist the company in judiciously deciding on the "make or buy" policy for semi-finished raw material.

Lean business processes, as a result of the above initiatives, would be saving both cost and time, right from receiving the enquiry from the customer through the delivery of the final products; enabling investment in suitable new manufacturing equipment through an effective CAPEX system; introducing cost control philosophy throughout the organization; enabling PTL to start activities like "Kaizen," the value-based management technique that ensures continuous improvement in teamwork, discipline, morale, and product quality; allowing the use of statistical tools to analyze and control the production process in line with the modern manufacturing techniques.

Stage 11: Strategy Implementation and Refinement

In Stage 11, the pivotal focus was on the meticulous implementation of the action plan, recognizing that execution is the linchpin for sustaining growth. Continuous monitoring and evaluation of this implementation were deemed critical for success. To ensure efficacy, a systematic approach was adopted, beginning with an assessment of the existing strategies to ascertain their impact. If results fell short, an examination followed to identify potential deficiencies in execution. If poorly executed, the scrutiny extended to communication effectiveness and validation of underlying assumptions.

Corrective action, if necessary, delved into the examination of alternate scenarios, ensuring that all facets were clearly defined and assessed. It was recognized that an inaccurate diagnosis of the current situation and crucial trends could lead to failure. Further investigation explored the alignment of supporting functional strategies with overall business unit strategies, ensuring consistency. Inconsistencies at this level could impede the desired strategic outcomes.

Simultaneously, the Sub-Teams established in Stage 10 continued their efforts to identify loose ends, uncover bottlenecks and enhance overall productivity. The Core Team at PTL championed the implementation of improvements across functional areas, including Marketing, R&D, Production, and Support Functions.

The structured implementation aligned with the "Functional Organization Structure," where the command and reporting lines were separated functionally.

Marketing Focus

Assisted by Frost & Sullivan, an external agency, the Core Team diligently analyzed the market size within the gearbox industry. Frost & Sullivan conducted an extensive market survey specific to the gearbox industry, aiming to project future growth and assess the potential competition that PTL might encounter from both local and multinational companies. The findings shed light on the anticipated growth rate of the gearbox industry market, taking into account the correlation with GDP growth. This strategic collaboration enabled PTL's leadership to gain precise insights into the market size, categorizing it into three essential components: Total Addressable Market (TAM), Serviceable Available Market (SAM), and Serviceable Obtainable Market (SOM).

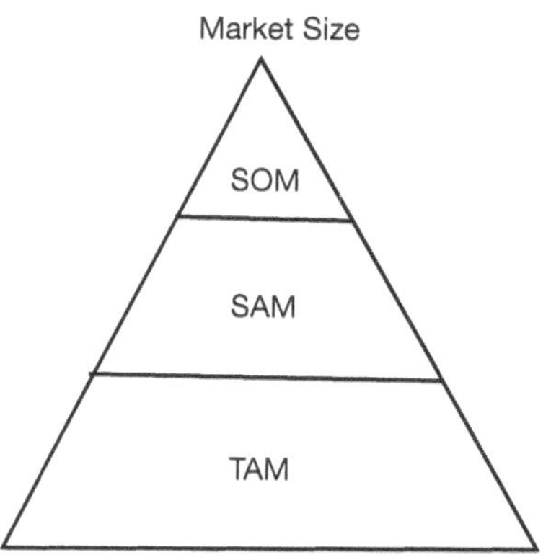

Fig. 14 Market Size

TAM: Total addressable market represents the entirety of the market potential.

SAM: Serviceable and available market signifies the portion of the market that is realistically reachable and serviceable.

SOM: Serviceable and obtainable market identifies the market segment that is not only serviceable but also realistically obtainable by PTL.

The industry survey also unveiled the market share of key competitors, allowing PTL to position itself strategically.

Table 5: Company Standing in the Industry

Main Competitors	Turnover Base Year (INR Million)	Market Share %
Premium Transmission	3,450	32
Shanthi Gears	970	9
Elecon Engineers	4,420	41
Flenders (Siemens)	750	7
NAW	540	5
Others	660	6

(Source: PTL Internal Records)

The Marketing sub-team worked on the Strengths and Weaknesses of PTL's major competitors to plan the company's strategy to attain enhanced profitability and growth. The SWOT of major competitors is presented below.

Elecon Engineers Ltd.

Strengths: Good investment in manufacturing facility, technical tie-up with some (four) international leaders, product range, aesthetics of final product and leadership position in Helical.

Weaknesses: Market reach, not consistent in customer dealings, owner-driven company.

Flender Drives Pvt. Ltd.

Strengths: International brand, pioneer in big and higher rated gearboxes, strong in cement and steel industry, huge product range.

Weaknesses: Delivery delay, market reach, after-sales service, and less flexible for customized products.

Shanti Gears Ltd.

Strengths: Low material cost, strong design team, versatile manufacturing, strong material handling, specialization in wind-mill gearboxes, competes in cost and quality of final products.

Weaknesses: High manpower turnover, no focused after-sales, future direction not clear, inadequate skill / quality of workforce.

NAW

Strengths: Focused on small Helical and geared motors, willingness to compete in pricing.

Weakness: Inflexible in offering customized product/s.

In response to the SWOT Analysis, PTL initiated corrective actions, addressing the areas of improvement and leveraging its own strengths. The initiatives included revamping the customer complaint register, improving job sequencing to minimize disturbances in the production schedule, and analyzing net margins for each customer order. The process was refined further by instituting a committee to approve priority changes in deliveries for customized products and jointly approving Gear Assembly (GA) drawings by both Marketing and R&D.

The Marketing sub-team also set immediate objectives to enhance sales and streamline processes, addressing customer complaints and pricing issues. Monthly plans for purchase and production were streamlined, and industry-specific initiatives were undertaken to tap into turnkey projects. The vital marketing information became an integral part of the Monthly Information System (MIS) presented to the CEO and the Board. Additionally, key result areas (KRAs) for the Vice President-Marketing, and territory managers were realigned and redrafted to ensure alignment with strategic goals.

Accordingly, a new process chart for customized and out-of-catalogue orders was formulated as follows:

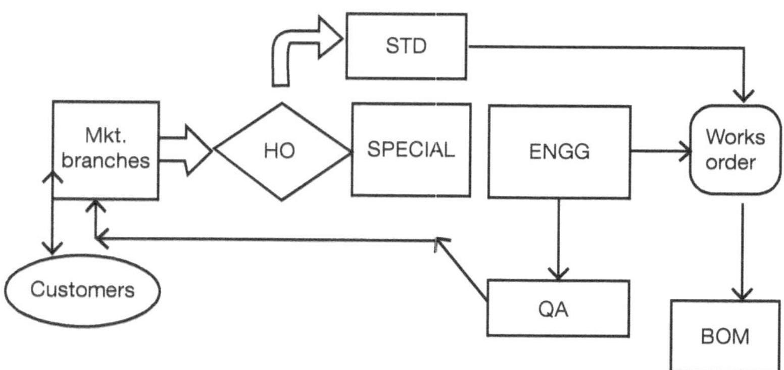

QA = Quality Assurance
QAP = QA Pricing
STD = Standard Specification Order
SPECIAL = Special Specification Order
BOM = Bill of Material
HO = Head Office
N.B Once customer accepts the QAP & conveys the acceptance
to Marketing Branch Office, it follows STD order route.

Fig. 15 Revised Process Chart for Standard and Special Orders

(Source: Outcome of ConsultMent Process at PTL)

These strategic steps ensured that the marketing team was well-equipped to offer value propositions to customers, aligning offerings with customer needs and ultimately enhancing the financial outcomes for both the company and its customers.

At PTL, the Core Team started finding out their own loose ends and started taking corrective actions.

1.   The team started with a complaint register for customers. The format was changed, and the same required a counter signature from both marketing and production departments so that

the seriousness of promptly resolving complaints would be understood and acted upon by both the departments concerned. Also, it was decided that a copy of customer complaints would be shared with R&D for product improvements. In addition, suitable backup records were initiated for recording the corrective action taken and time lapsed.

2. Disturbance in the production schedule due to haphazard delivery schedule committed by Marketing was minimized by improved job sequencing done by the newly formed cross-functional team.

3. Steps were taken to work out product-wise net margin in each customer order so that change in priority, if any, would be based on how well the price was negotiated.

4. It was noticed that the priority of supply in case of specialized or customized products was often changed by the marketing engineers and that disturbed the R&D's rhythm and also upset the production cycle. It was decided that "Priority changes" in delivery, if any, had to be first approved by the newly formed three-member committee, having representatives from Marketing, R&D, and Production departments.

5. It was noticed that the Gear Assembly (GA) drawings done by the marketing engineers were inaccurate. It was decided that the GA drawing had to be jointly approved by both Marketing and R&D before releasing it to Production. The benefits expected from the said improvements were as follows:

   i. The process of feedback from the Marketing department to R&D and Manufacturing departments regarding customer complaints and pricing would become robust.

    ii. Customer complaint analysis would be done using statistical tools.

    iii. Product promotion and productivity would be improved.

6. Certain immediate objectives for the marketing team were set up: Increase the sale of Extruder Gearboxes by 90% from the present base; increase the sale of Fluid Couplings by 50%; increase the sale of Planetary Gearboxes by 30% from the present level of sales, with reduction of time by 70% in releasing the bill of material (BOM) for non-standard gearboxes. This would correct the product mix and improve the net-margin/ profit for PTL.

7. It was noticed that the monthly plan for purchase and production (customer orders) was delayed by the Marketing department. It was decided that VP-Marketing, would personally ensure the availability of the "Final Plan" a week prior to the commencement of the month. This would enable Production and Purchase to plan their activities.

8. The industry survey also revealed that PTL was losing out on large orders from turnkey projects because PTL's marketing team overlooked consultants and contractors who normally place orders in such cases. Necessary steps were initiated to plug this void.

9. Based on the above, vital marketing information became a part of the MIS (monthly information system), which is placed before the CEO and the Board. Also, key result areas (KRA's) of Vice President, Marketing, and his territory managers were re-aligned and re-drafted suitably.

These steps would enable the marketing team to offer value propositions to the customer, based on the understanding of the customer need and developing a unique mix of offering to suit the customer requirements and in turn improve financials of both the company and the customer.

Focus on Technological Advancements in Production

1. The sub-team initiated a path toward technical excellence through a series of strategic steps. Pivotal decisions made by the cross-sectional Core Team regarding achieving manufacturing excellence were effectively communicated to all the employees across the four plants.

2. The plant staff undertook the task of assessing the productivity of each machine and identifying idle machinery that needed disposal.

3. The authority to make decisions about acquiring new machines was decentralized to each plant under the overall supervision of the CEO. Respective plant engineers were entrusted with the responsibility of finalizing capital expenditures for their respective plants, fostering ownership and accountability for improved productivity.

4. In alignment with the revised organizational structure, where the Production function now fell under the direct purview of a technically-equipped CEO, the fourth step involved instructing the GMs of the plants to focus specifically on certain targets during the next capital expenditure. These targets included a 35% increase in the assembly capacity of Helical gearboxes, enhancing casting capability to accommodate an additional business volume of INR 6000

million and improving the aesthetic appeal and packing of various products.

5. The assessment and control of productivity, rework, and wastages were transferred to an enhanced SAP system, with a dedicated Systems Manager overseeing the responsibility. This shift allowed for a more transparent and effective application of both motivational and corrective measures, enhancing the quality and reliability of PTL's end products.

6. As a short-term measure, the sixth step introduced CpK (Process Capability Index) to evaluate the mechanical process capability across all plants.

7. This step involved the implementation of OEE (Overall Equipment Effectiveness) index, encompassing productivity, quality, and machine downtime for long-term benefits. This facilitated the use of VSM (Value Stream Mapping) for achieving desired results.

8. This step aimed to measure the Total Business Process through the formation of a three-member team, comprising representatives from technical, marketing and finance. This team focused on measuring the Cycle Time, covering all activities from customer inquiry to supplying finished products per customer specifications, known as VSD (Value Stream Design). To enhance meaningful control, the entire VSD was subdivided on a plant-wise basis.

The cumulative measures taken for long-term benefits included improved productivity, minimized rework, and reduced wastage of material and manpower. Modernization of the existing equipment with the latest technology and the identification and removal of bottlenecks in the supply chain were crucial. Additionally, the implementation of backward integration, such as establishing Centrifugal Casting Process, aimed to make products more cost-effective and improve quality and delivery time. The focus on core operations like grinding, assembling, painting, packing, and subcontracting, along with specific mechanisms for "make or buy" decisions, further streamlined the operations.

Short-term goals included a 30% reduction in manufacturing costs for the "Modular Helical Series" of gearboxes and a 25% reduction for "PVC Couplings," benchmarked against the immediate industry competitors.

The CEO's message to the Production employees was unequivocal: "Put your personal touch on the job. Contemplate ways to enhance your product – a memory of which will bring the customer back to your company."

Business Processes Enhancement

Business Process Management involves addressing intricate challenges throughout the entire product life cycle, spanning design, execution, and continuous improvement. The goal is to streamline and optimize these processes to align with the dynamic business environment. Establishing improved and restructured internal connections between Staff Functions (Finance, HR, R&D, ERP) and Line Functions (Production, Marketing) is a pivotal step towards achieving the envisioned "Level Next."

The PTL-specific staff function needed the following improvements:

SAP Utilization: The SAP system, serving as an ERP tool at PTL, was identified as being underutilized. It became evident that crucial information, such as the cost of rework/rerun, production process wastages, comparative costs of outsourcing versus in-house manufacturing, and the valuation of slow-moving and non-moving inventory, was either unavailable or unreliable in some areas. Necessary measures were implemented to activate the SAP functions, ensuring the extraction of essential details for the implementation of activity-based management (ABM) controls.

Costing Optimization: Recognizing the urgency of acquiring accurate data for "outsourced components" versus "in-house manufacturing," the costing team was tasked with compiling essential data to support "make or buy" decisions. An improved costing system not only aids in decision-making but also contributes to new product development, design optimization, and the implementation of Value Engineering at every stage of product development.

Financial Fine-tuning: Building on the benchmarking conducted in the previous stage, financial processes were fine-tuned to focus on operating margin, monitor waste and rework in production, optimize inventory management, and provide an enhanced Management Information System (MIS) on a monthly basis. This timely and improved MIS facilitates proactive corrective actions.

Human Resources Strategic Focus

Before the implementation of this strategic initiative, HR activities primarily centered around Industrial Relations (IR) issues.

Recognizing the need for a comprehensive HR strategy, the HR head was entrusted with expanding its scope into the following key areas:

1. Skills Enhancement: Assess and implement programs to upgrade employee skill sets through on-the-job training and assisted education programs.

2. Employee Engagement: Launch a reward scheme to encourage employees to provide practical suggestions for product and process improvement, fostering team spirit.

3. Career Development: Revamp and institute transparent policies for internal career development, job rotation (for multi-skilling), and cash rewards for outstanding contributions.

4. Performance Management: Commence goal setting on an employee-wise basis and improve the annual performance appraisal system.

5. Salary Structure Enhancement: Revise the salary structure for white-collar employees, to align with industry best practices.

6. Innovation Promotion: Recruit 2nd/3rd level engineers in the R&D team to support succession planning and actively seek suitable executives, even considering talent acquisition from rival companies.

7. Special Salary Structure for R&D: Plan and implement a revised/special salary structure for the R&D department.

8. Campus Recruitment: Set up arrangements with leading engineering colleges for recruiting fresh engineers on a regular basis.

The revitalized HR function is expected to enhance the following:

- Skill set assessment and training for employees' skill set upgrades.
- Periodical Employee Satisfaction Surveys.
- Recruitment, retention, and promotion of the best employees.
- Establishment and maintenance of a conducive and transparent work atmosphere across the organization.
- Creation of a desirable work culture, open to learning and unlearning.
- Establishment of a recognition system to boost innovation in both products and processes.

These initiatives are anticipated to improve morale and motivation among employees and aid the management in finding and retaining top talent, paving the way for effective succession planning. Implemented under the STAR process, these initiatives contribute to PTL's journey to the Next Level. To monitor the progress, various feedback forms were also introduced by the company.

(See Exhibits 1 to 4: Feedback forms introduced by HR at PTL - Measuring Work Challenges, Employee Training and Development, Competencies Mapping, and People Management Challenges.)

Strategic Procurement Focus

Quoting David Hutchins from his book, *Just in Time: Strategies for Material Resource Planning*, "Just in Time is not just stock control or quality circles – to succeed, it requires the commitment and enthusiasm of all employees. The concept of Just in Time has gradually evolved, sending a message that organizations should prioritize the 'procurement process,' and the 'product' will naturally follow." Effective procurement is not just about buying goods and services; it's about strategically managing the supply chain to drive overall business success.

In manufacturing companies like PTL, the Purchase function plays a pivotal role in enhancing the organization's bottom line. Procurements encompass both raw materials and semi-finished goods that eventually become integral parts of the final product. As part of the STAR initiative, PTL established the Procurement and Product Planning Cell (PPC), comprising representatives from procurement, marketing, and production departments. The purpose was to delve into Value Stream Mapping for expedited delivery, ranging from vendor selection to procuring high-quality raw materials at optimal costs. The PPC aimed to synergize materials planning and industrial engineering across all four plants, targeting a 20 to 25 percent reduction in the Lead Time (from order booking to delivery) across all product lines.

The scope of the initiative included the following:

1. Project Planning: Creating an activity breakdown and time-bound project plan.
2. Dispatch Plan Monitoring: Regular monitoring of daily dispatch plans.

3. Supplier Engagement: Involving suppliers in the product development plan.

4. Process Optimization: Identifying and eliminating non-value-added processes.

5. On-Time Delivery: Ensuring on-time delivery of subcontracted materials.

6. Vendor Base Enhancement: Expanding the vendor base, particularly for Foundry items.

7. Payment Optimization: Ensuring on-time payments to suppliers and renegotiating for an overall 8% to 12% reduction in purchase costs.

8. Centralized Procurements: Centralizing procurements of "A" category inventory items based on the ABC Analysis Technique for Inventory Management.

9. Decision Analysis: Introduction of robust analysis to support "make or buy" decisions, enhancing outsourcing capability to include analysis, simulation, and optimization of processes, along with the ability to manipulate, combine and recombine product and process designs.

To complement these improvements, it was essential to streamline the flow of materials from preparing the bill of materials to the point of dispatch to the ultimate customer. A revised material flow chart was developed to facilitate this process.

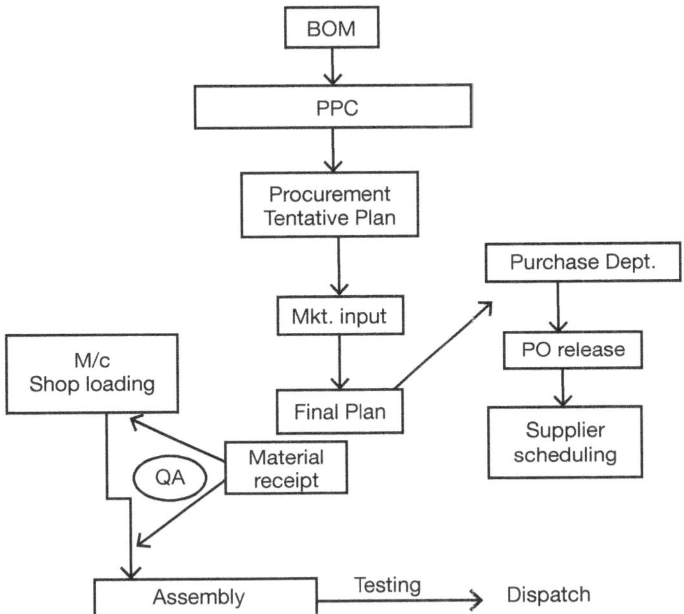

Fig. 16 Revised Material Flow Chart

(Source: Outcome of ConsultMent process at PTL)

The progress made thus far empowered the Core Team to embark on the final stage of developing a roadmap to achieve a sustainable growth plan.

•••

Chapter 6

Writing Up Your Consolidated Business Plan (The Roadmap of Growth)

Stage 12 The Roadmap of Growth

The strategic process that far, as intended, worked as a wakeup call, and for the revitalized group of employees, it was a new day, new products, new processes, new markets, and new possibilities. PTL's Core Team not only readied themselves to actualize the mission but also kept their colleagues and juniors informed about the positive changes happening in the organization to regain the apex position in the gear manufacturing market and that soon the company would hit INR 10,000 million in sales. The entire organization was now concentrating on improving the effectiveness of the 5 M's of business: Money, Machines, Men, Material, and Market. Having positioned the company for all-round growth, the inspired and motivated employees started with a positive frame of mind to construct a five-year pragmatic roadmap that would lead to actualizing the company's mission. Aptly quoted, "Success is a manifestation of good luck that results from inspiration, aspiration, desperation, and perspiration; generally in that sequence." The threadbare discussions and implementation of all-round improvements in each functional area led to the foundation of the five-year roadmap. What had seemed impossible till then, now seemed definitely doable.

PTL being one of the seasoned and major players in the gearbox industry in India, the company had considerable knowledge about the local market. Also, the survey conducted by Frost & Sullivan gave deeper insights into the Indian market along with authenticated data. To achieve the dream growth, PTL had to become a major exporter in the growing global market. To tap this opportunity, suitable study and analysis were inevitable to target some regions in the international market.

The Export Market

Alain Gomez, CEO, Thomson SA, says "You do not choose to become global. The market chooses for you; it forces your hand." PTL planned to expand into the foreign market with a view to gaining access to new customers; fully capturing economies of scale, which promotes the learning curve effects, and thereby improving sustainability; leveraging its competencies and capabilities into a position of competitive advantage in foreign markets and spreading its business risk across a wider market base.

The process of tapping a suitable international market started with gathering relevant information from various sources. After the market survey, the attention was shifted to regions where PTL's products and after-sales services could be effectively deployed. The steps so far enabled the company to finalize the "focus regions." The targeted regions emerged based on the customers' requirements in respective regions, types of industry segments that operated in that region, the level of existing competition in those regions, possible price range prevailing for PTL's products, the growth rate of the chosen industry segment and lastly, the analysis of strengths and weaknesses of PTL's products vis-à-vis competitors' products. To start with, PTL decided to keep the manufacturing base only in India (a one-country production base) and to open sales and service centers in focused regions. Eventually, depending on the country's prospects, PTL would decide to launch the production base through either deploying a licensee or franchisee or having strategic alliances with local manufacturers or going by the joint-venture route.

Based on the said steps, PTL could finalize the target industries that can use their Gearboxes and the regions where the company's products can penetrate. The industries targeted were Cement, Iron & Steel, Mining, Sugar, Rubber & Plastic, and Power generation. The key regions selected for the export were Africa, the Middle East, Central Europe, South America, and South East Asia. Accordingly, a region-wise export breakup was prepared as follows:

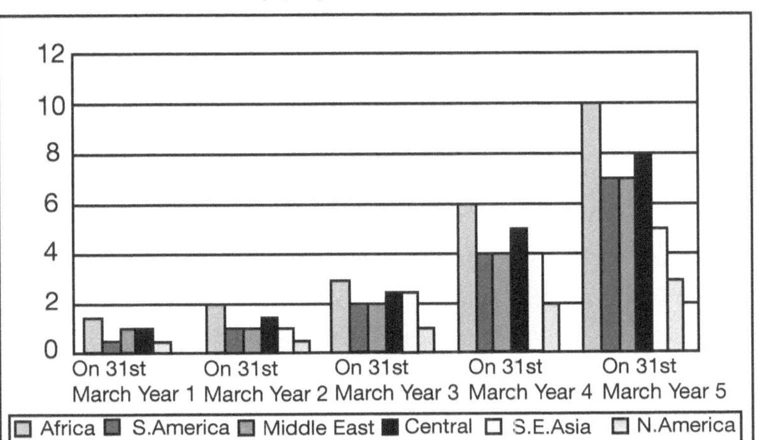

	On 31st March Year 1	On 31st March Year 2	On 31st March Year 3	On 31st March Year 4	On 31st March Year 5
Africa	1.5	2	3	6	10
S. America	0.5	1	2	4	7
Middle East	1	1	2	4	7
Central Europe	1	1.5	2.5	5	8
S.E. Asia	0.5	1	2.5	4	5
N. America	0	0.5	1	2	3
Total	4.5	7	13	25	40

Fig. 17 Roadmap (Region-wise Export)

(Source: PTL internal sources)

The identified products of the company that were found suitable for the above-mentioned industries were Fluid Coupling, Geared Motors, Cooling Towers, Extruder Gearbox, Planetary, and a specific range of Helical and Worm Gearboxes. To support and push planned export, an export marketing team was identified. This team was a sub-set of the Corporate Marketing located at the head office. The team further analyzed the region-wise export market and finalized their strategy to achieve the sales target through appointing Liaison officers and Dealers in those identified regions. The study revealed that the Africa Region would be the most fertile. Accordingly, the overview of the Africa region, depicting products, dealer network, and intended strategy was worked out as follows:

Findings of the Region	Company's Strategy
<ul><li>Countries – 54</li><li>GDP growth forecast from existing 4.5% to 5.1% & 5.4% in 2012, 2013 respectively.</li><li>Economy based on Mining, Agriculture, Manufacturing services.</li><li>Northern and Southern Africa form a major portion of the GDP.</li><li>Major imports from Germany, UK, USA, France, China, and Japan.</li></ul>	<ul><li>Countries under focus – Republic of South Africa / Zambia / Nigeria.</li><li>Presently, PTL has a Sales Agent located at Johannesburg looking after the entire Africa. The plan is to have representation at Nigeria and Zambia by 2013.</li><li>At present, one distributor at South Africa & Zambia is supplying PTL products to the Mining industry. The future plan is to appoint distributors in North and South African regions by 2014.</li></ul>

• David Brown, SEW, Flender, Sumitomo, Nord, and Hansen have well-established marketing networks spread throughout Africa. • David Brown has a manufacturing facility in SA. • Flender and SEW supply from their Chinese plants. • Preference for European / US brands. • Price / Quality / Aesthetics / Delivery sensitive OEM market. • Equally distributed OEM and Reseller market.	• Focus on Mining / Sugar / Steel industry. • Focus on Mill duty reducers – E-mills / planetary and large size helical. • Introduction of power skids consisting of medium size helical, fluid coupling, base frame. • Developing stockists for geared motors and fluid couplings by 2013. • Developing service support network by 2014. • Establishment of a logistics hub in Johannesburg by 2015.

After the completion of the export strategy, the Core Team started work on the total business strategy for achieving the goal.

Consolidated Business Plan

Having worked on the newly targeted export market together with the updated knowledge on the local market, the final fine-tuned product-wise target was developed by the Core Team.

The product-wise final plan emerged as follows:

Table 6: Budgeted Product-wise Sales Breakup

(INR Lakhs excluding Excise)

Group	On 31st March Year 1	On 31st March Year 2	On 31st March Year 3	On 31st March Year 4	On 31st March Year 5
Worm	12380	12660	13380	14700	18965
Lift Machine	620	1200	2000	3500	4515
Helical	12195	13802	17230	24935	32170
Planetary	1500	2100	3300	4200	5420
Fluid Coupling	3750	5320	7080	10000	12900
Spares	2540	3750	4650	5810	7495
Geared Motor	2825	4250	6540	8500	10965
Auto Trans	2200	2600	3250	3700	4770
Total	**38010**	**45682**	**57430**	**75345**	**100000**

	On 31st March Year 1	On 31st March Year 2	On 31st March Year 3	On 31st March Year 4	On 31st March Year 5
Export	-	2750	5350	10250	18000
Domestic	-	42532	51580	64095	79200
Spares	-	400	500	1000	1800

(Source: PTL Internal Records)

The product-wise plan enabled PTL to understand when and where to market; what will be the product breakup to be loaded in four plants; what is expected from each supporting function and at what time and quantity; the clarity on the level of purchases, storage, and finances required along with planning on Vendor Base required to meet the increasing demand and activity level.

It was now required to establish the overall picture to be presented to stakeholders. Accordingly, the consolidated position of targeted sales, starting with comparable actuals for the year 2010-11 (base year), were worked out. Contributions of local sales and export sales were depicted separately for more clarity. Accordingly, year-wise targeted sales along with CAGR were prepared as follows:

Table 7: Summary of Target Sales Plan

Particulars	Actual (INR in Millions)	Short-Term (INR in Millions)			Long-Term (INR in Millions)		CAGR
Year	Base Year	On 31st March Year 1	On 31st March Year 2	On 31st March Year 3	On 31st March Year 4	On 31st March Year 5	%
Local Sales	3004	3711	4253	5158	6410	7920	20.90%
Exports	153	60	275	535	1025	1800	63.70%
Spares	43	30	40	50	100	280	-
Total	**3200**	**3801**	**4568**	**5743**	**7535**	**10000**	**24.80%**

(Source: PTL Internal Records)

Based on the said target and considering the improvements implemented by PTL, the positively charged and motivated team was expected to improve EBIDTA from 19.3% of sales (at base year) to 37% of sales (in the target year), as detailed below:

Table 8: PTL's Expected Financials for the Target Year (Fifth Year)

{INR Million}

Premium Energy Transmission Ltd.		
Particulars	**Rs.**	**%**
Gross Sales		
Excise duty		
Net Sales	10,000	
Other Income		
Net Revenue	10,000	100%
Raw Material	3900	39.0%
Employee Cost	700	7.0%
Other Mfg. Expenses	1000	10.0%
Selling & admin. Expenses	700	7.0%
Total expenditure	6300	63.0%
EBIDTA	3700	37.0%
Interest		
Depreciation		
Profit Before Tax		
Tax Provision		
Profit After Tax		

(Source: Outcome of ConsultMent Process at PTL)

In short, strategy formulation is all about securing growth and sustainability in the future. All progressive companies develop a clear vision for the next 5-10 years. The initiative taken so far at PTL in terms of boosting innovation and expanding the export market would lead the company to the expected CAGR of 24.8% despite competition from multinationals. The series of steps taken in cost effectiveness and improvised business process controls would reduce the raw material consumption to 39% of sales. Learning and shared vision at the individual and team level along with management techniques of improvisation are expected to improve productivity and reduce employee cost to 7% in terms of increased sales. Effective implementation, formation of cross-functional teams, and teamwork would reduce manufacturing, selling, and administrative costs and improve internal linkages. Given the high quality of the strategy-making process, the knowledge of peripheral vision (giving early warnings) is expected to improve PTL's EBITDA to around 37%.

End Note on the Strategic Process at PTL

The Strategic Process through the STAR initiative at PTL sharpened the focus on the company's goal, assisted in upgrading employees' skill sets, developed team spirit, and infused positivity throughout the organization. The CEO made the thoughtful decision to conduct the strategic initiative through the Core Team and flawlessly executed the planned strategy to differentiate from competitors and attain the company's mission. The seamless process followed at PTL indeed created a changed company.

The typical timeframe for the creation of the Winning Team and introduction of the Strategic Process in your company would approximately take 18 weeks, as detailed below:

STAGES	TIME FRAME
1. CEO's Initial Interaction	2 Weeks
2. The Action Plan	3rd Week
3. Formation of the Core Team	4th Week
4. Assimilation of the Core Team	5th Week
5. Addressing the Pain Areas	6th Week
6. Unified Team with Common Goals	---- *
7. SWOT Analysis	7th & 8th Week
8. Restructuring the Organization	9th Week
9. Preparing to be Future-ready	10th Week
10. Focus Areas and Benchmarking	11th & 12th Week
11. Implementation of the Action Plan	13th to 16th Week
12. Writing your Roadmap of Growth	17th & 18th Week

*Outcome of the first five stages

The active involvement of the Core Team in the decision-making process (STAR process) enabled them to own the process. The strategic process enabled them to write an achievable Business Plan, a strategic path toward gaining Competitive Advantage.

•••

Part III
Exploring Differentiators

Part III of the book deals with impactful differentiators that contribute to the increased profitability of the company in the constantly evolving world of business. The case-study analyses of many successful Indian companies are included to understand the relative role of each differentiator in business growth.

A Recap

We started our journey of understanding Strategic Management by familiarizing ourselves with the evolution of the concept of Competitive Advantage (Part I). Chapter 1 summarized the changing business landscape, and Chapter 2 revealed various new trends and concepts that had proved effective in the past. The knowledge gained enlarged our understanding of the concept of Competitive Advantage spanning four decades. We realized that the Competitive Management theory is continuously evolving and remains in a paradigm state.

In Part II, we learned how a "Winning Team" was shaped in PTL. We also got familiar with various stages through which the strategic process gets defined, shaped, implemented, and practiced. The learning so far may help you implement such strategies in your own company to gain sustainable competitive advantage over your rivals.

Introduction

We shall now analyze what the differentiators are and how they are deployed to enhance profitability. Later, we shall consider the researched outcome from live cases of some of the successful Indian companies to understand the role of differentiators impacting their business growth.

Differentiators are an integral part of the strategic process, and often, they work in tandem. Some of the differentiators were found to be more relevant and important, depending on the complex nature of the business environment in which a company operates. It is important to identify impactful differentiators in your unique business setup and deploy them effectively to enhance growth and generate a healthier bottom line.

Differentiators

Differentiation is a business strategy whereby companies attempt to gain a competitive advantage. Differentiators enable companies to increase the perceived value of their products relative to the perceived value of competitors' products, create unique selling points (USPs), craft and execute the right strategy, improve the relevance of the firm's actions to attract customers, hire good brains, improve productivity, introduce efficient business processes, embark upon cost reduction, and ultimately increase the returns to the shareholders.

•••

Chapter 7

Focusing on Impactful Differentiators

Today's crowded market is getting more competitive by the day. Companies do not have a choice but to differentiate in ways that are relevant to customers. The differentiators have to be such that they are defensible against the competitors' encroachment. Analysis of many progressive Indian and multinational companies revealed some impactful differentiators contributing to their success, in spite of facing fierce global competition. The important differentiators that emerged from the research are described below.

i)   **Market Leadership**

Market leadership is the position of the company with the largest market share and highest profitability margin in a given market for goods and services. Market share may be measured by either the volume of goods sold or the value of those goods. Companies focusing on market leadership strive to keep themselves ahead of their industry rivals by successfully deploying winning pricing mechanism, introducing effective supply chain management and increasing the valuation of their brand (as observed in HLL).

ii) **Innovations**

The traditional Competitive Advantage Theory considered only product innovation as a differentiator. However, subsequent research found a variety of forms of innovation such as innovative ways of reducing product cost, introduction of lean business processes and reducing waste of material and time, improvement in business models (as observed in Dell) and social responsibilities (as observed in TISCO).

iii) **Cost Efficiency**

The companies that focus on cost leadership have a minimum cost per unit of production, along with lower finance costs and lower overheads in comparison to the industry standard, and are more prosperous in matured markets (as observed in Canon, India).

iv) **Business Process Management (BPM)**

BPM enables companies to solve complex problems and contributes to corporate sustainability, innovation, and growth. BPM provides the capability to manage the entire life cycle of the change management process from design to development to execution to continuous improvement and strengthens the internal linkages through an effective use of MIS and ERP (as observed in Xerox).

v) **Learning Organization (at an individual and team level)**
Managers at all levels keep upgrading skill sets and amending their own attitude along with that of their team members to match the changing business environment, customer preference, and industry regulations. Skill sets are upgraded through learning, creating, leading, and changing both individually and collectively (as observed in Intel).

vi) **Quality of the firm's strategy-making process**
The strategy-making process has many interlinked elements such as vision and mission, analysis of internal and external environment, making strategic choices, implementation, and achieving competitive advantage. Business decisions and actions emerging from this chain of activities are required to be interconnected and coordinated to achieve a coherent overall strategy (as observed in PTL).

vii) **Use of management tools and techniques**
There are many proven techniques such as Core Competencies, Benchmarking, Balanced Scorecard and Six-Sigma. It is seen that successful companies often use these techniques to their advantage in strategizing.

viii) **Ability and Creativity of the Top Management**
The mental ability of an effective leader flips between two different modes – thinking and representing – which enable him/her to deal with a greater range of ambiguous and complex possibilities.

In a worldwide research with over 1500 CEOs, creativity was identified as the most important leadership competency for organizations seeking competitive advantage in the contemporary business. A creative person strives for introspection with his self and fosters creativity throughout the organization with two dimensions: the individual and the collective.

A creative mind with the power to predict enables your company to accomplish its goals by continuously matching real-time events with historical patterns to improve business process. Such analysis can also advise on what it will take to align the company's resources, technology, and culture to an unstoppable, world-class business (as observed in various Fortune 500 companies).

ix) **Intrapreneurship and Teamwork**

"Intrapreneurs" or "Corporate Entrepreneurs" are professionals working within the organization who turn ideas into profit. They do all that an entrepreneur does, with the exception of taking the financial risk.

The role played by mid-level managers in transforming their teams to great heights has been established beyond doubt. However, it is imperative for the team as a whole to understand that, each one of them has both, a responsibility and an obligation to perform (as observed in Praj Industries).

x) **Implementation of Strategy**

Executing the strategy is anchored by pragmatic and compelling conceptual framework: building the resource strength and organizational capabilities needed to execute the strategy in a competent fashion; allocating ample resources to strategy-critical activities; ensuring that policies and procedures facilitate rather than impede strategy execution; instituting best practices and pushing for continuous improvement in how value chain activities are performed; installing information and operating systems that enable company personnel to better carry out their strategic roles proficiently; tying rewards and incentives directly to the achievement of performance targets and good strategy execution; shaping the work environment and corporate culture to fit the overall strategy; and exerting the internal leadership needed to drive implementation forward (as observed in Andalan Paper & Pulp).

xi) **Developed Peripheral Vision**

The periphery – that fuzzy zone at the edge of an organization's focus – is where early signals of both threats and opportunities are sensed. Real-time peripheral vision gives companies the ability to monitor and react to changes and address problems as they occur. In future, successful companies must be able to recognize what is coming early enough to take evasive action or steer toward an emerging opportunity. Vigilant organizations adopt an inquisitive approach to strategy that alerts them to possible changes from the periphery, make the necessary investment in the knowledge systems and analytical support and assign clear accountability for detecting, tracking and sharing weak signals (as observed in Bharat Forge).

xii) **Strategic Restructuring and Disinvestment Policies**

In a competitive world, resources are rather scarce, and firms require flexibility, speed, and economies of scale to stand hyper competition. To achieve the said objectives, firms need to constantly position themselves through acquisitions, joint ventures and alliances with strategically suitable companies (as observed in Jet Airways and Indigo alliance for ground staff).

•••

Chapter 8
Role of Differentiators

That Differentiation is a high level of discriminator (among companies) is known; however, the impact of each differentiator in a company's success is not easy to judge and understand. This chapter tries to address the said impediment by researching the live Strategic Process that actually evolved in some progressive Indian companies. We shall analyze the role played by different differentiators and understand which of them proved more impactful in the given situation. Later, we shall establish the relationship between the deployed differentiators and enhancement of profitability through statistical inference.

Research findings on the importance of differentiators

The business environment for every organization is complex. There are many external factors affecting your business organization such as customers and their changing needs, suppliers and their priorities, market trends, economics, regulations, technology, demographics, and competitors. Also, the organization is influenced internally by the quality of people and their skill sets, effectiveness of systems, the ability to strategize, employee culture, organizational structures, business processes, clarity in goal setting, and the values attached.

The complexities and ever-changing interrelated realities of business are depicted below:

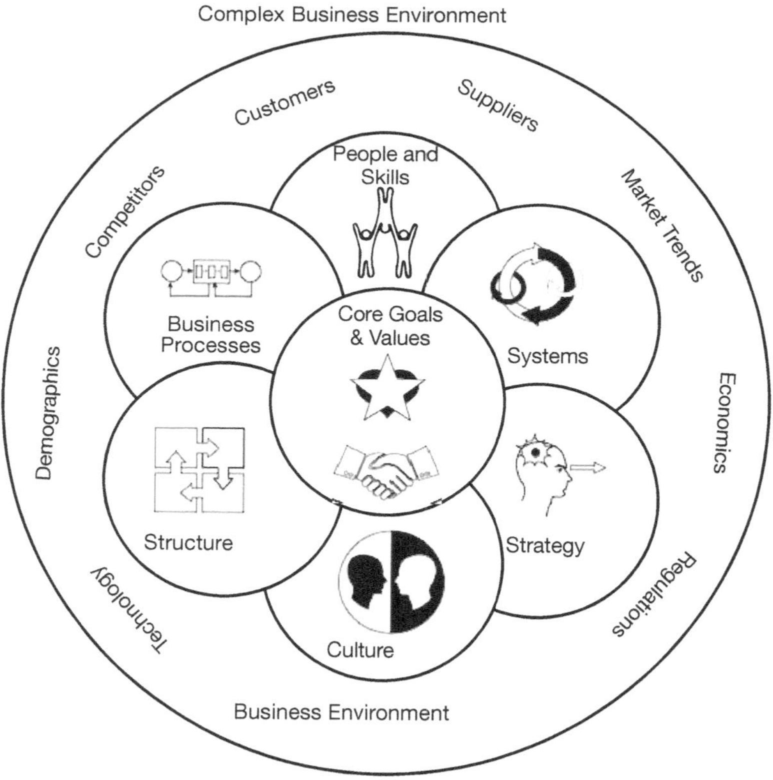

Fig. 18 Gelinas-James Elements of Organization Model

The role and impact of various differentiators in a complex business environment would be clear after studying some of the live cases. Such case analysis of the deployed differentiators in select companies would enable us to obtain a fair and balanced reflection of the industry on the role of differentiators and their impact on profitability and growth. Let us start examining some of the Indian (large & SME) companies who have been successful in the fiercely competitive market.

(Names of the companies are used as they were during the research period.)

Premium Transmission Ltd. (PTL)

Nature of business

PTL has been engaged in manufacturing of mechanical power transmission products for over four decades. PTL has established its presence in a variety of product lines, viz. Worm gearbox; Helical & Bevel helical gearbox; Vertical Coal Pulverizing Mill gearbox; Planetary gearbox; Helical & Worm geared motors; Bevel Helical Cooling Tower gearbox; Fluid Coupling, both constant & variable speed; Extruder gearbox; Elevator machines; and Auto Components.

The role played by the major differentiators in enhancing the profitability and growth of PTL can be elaborated as follows:

Creativity and ability of the Management

The mental ability of an effective leader flips between two different modes − thinking and representing − which enable him/her to deal with a greater range of ambiguous and complex possibilities. The Board of Director's realization of the company's stagnation, timely appointment of a suitable CEO, and giving him a clearly-defined mandate along with the necessary authority and freedom to run the strategic initiative demonstrated their ability to deal with the company's crisis.

The creative persons (CEO and Core Team) strove for introspection and fostered creativity throughout the organization with two dimensions: the individual and the collective. The management team handled the delicate situation in a matured way by first understanding the undercurrents, introspecting on the problems faced, and judicially planning the STAR (Strategic Transformation for Achieving Desired Results) process to infuse positivity throughout the organization. The constitution of the core team, leadership development and succession planning, upgradation of skills, and participative and transparent management process ensured sustained competitive advantage for a long time. The well-timed and stage-by-stage development process, thoughtfully planned and effectively executed, amply showed creativity at the leadership level and at the management team level.

Quality of the firm's strategy-making process

Through the 12 stages (as given in Chapter 6), the PTL process revealed the following:

1. Timely action taken by the BOD to overcome stagnation
2. Empowering the CEO with suitable authority and defining an unambiguous mission statement
3. The CEO forming the core-team of cross-sectional employees to drive strategic intent
4. Improving their morale and creating a unified team
5. Developing characteristics of an "excellent innovative company."

PTL demonstrated the quality of strategy-making and reaffirmed that it is a must for growth, performance, and change. As of date, despite slowing down of the Indian economy, PTL, growing at the highest (among rivals) CAGR of 17%, has divested from the Auto Unit, has acquired a German company, and is on course to actualize its Mission.

Intrapreneurship and teamwork

"Intrapreneurs" or "Corporate Entrepreneurs" are professionals working within the organizations who turn ideas into profit. They do all that an entrepreneur does, with the exception of taking the financial risk. PTL's CEO, after forming a suitable Core Team, allowed them to realize the problems faced by the company through case studies of some of the multinational companies, followed by making them air out grievances through an exercise of addressing pain areas. Also, the CEO's actions of changing the KRAs of key managers; raising the morale of the team through transparent processes; shaping professionals to turn ideas into profitable ventures; and guiding them to freely discuss, debate, and generate issue-based solutions were ideal examples of intrapreneurship.

The Core Team, on their part, enthusiastically upgraded their skill sets in the process and resolved interdepartmental frictions. The cross-functional team, including mid-level managers, gradually understood that each of them has both a responsibility and an obligation to perform. The team undertook the task to iron out drawbacks, improved productivity, and pushed the strategic initiative to give birth to the final roadmap for achieving the targeted mission. The initiative at PTL reaffirmed that the leadership at different levels in management and the demonstrated strength of teamwork are essential for growth, performance, and change.

Cost control

A vibrant and positively charged core team set in motion process innovation, which encompassed improving product quality, bringing in operational excellence, changing the business model, and all the other aspects of PTL's way of doing business.

Specific steps were undertaken such as SWOT analysis, BCG matrix, benchmarking, tech excellence, enhancing productivity, sharp business process, upgradation of skill sets, reduced wastages, streamlining business processes, and many more such improvisations that brought in cost consciousness and improved the profit margin.

Despite focusing on cost reduction and bringing in the characteristics of excellent innovative company, PTL never lost customer focus.

Nichrome India Pvt. Ltd. (NIPL)
Nature of business

NIPL specializes in manufacturing packaging machines and offers end-to-end solutions for packaging a variety of products worldwide. The company's Mission is "To become a dominant player in the Global Packaging Place by offering appropriate End-to-End Packaging Solutions." There are several factors impacting the choice of packaging, such as product behavior, characteristics of the packaging material, packaging style, pre and post-packaging systems, and so on.

The range of products manufactured by NIPL includes liquid and solid product packaging machines; packaging solutions for viscous products like pickles, tomato puree, fruit pulp, and jelly; aseptic packaging solutions; jar filling lines; processing machines; and specialized packaging material. As of date, the company's sales turnover is relatively modest, around INR 900 million; however, this does not deter the company from generously spending money on Research and Development. The company is known for manufacturing the first ever Flip-pack Machine in India, as also the path-breaking in-house development of "Nichrome Aseptic Pouch Packing System" for long shelf life products like milk and juices. The company now offers a range of pre and post packaging equipment like product handling systems, metal detectors, machine-fitted printers, pick-fill-seal solutions, bailing and cartoning systems, liquid processing equipment, and specialty packaging materials. NIPL has been growing at 30% CAGR on the sheer willpower to succeed, based on continuous innovation.

The role played by the major differentiators in enhancing the profitability and growth of NIPL can be elaborated as follows:

Innovations
Innovation has been a key message flowing throughout NIPL. All the new developments in products and manufacturing processes

are well supported and rewarded by the management. Developing customized packaging solutions is the real need of today's world, which is well imbibed at NIPL and actively encouraged at every level of management. Learning and skill upgradation is a constant activity and is supported by a professionally qualified management team. Engineers are also rewarded for improvements in processes, and promising engineers are regularly sent to international conferences and exhibitions to promote in-house innovations.

The Flip Pack machine was developed by NIPL for the first time in India in as early as 1982, followed by the development of Slid Packaging Machines (FFS m/c). Another path-breaking development took place in 2009 when the Aseptic Pouch Packing M/c was developed for long-shelf life products like milk and juices. The earlier machines had a production capacity of 1,500 pouches per hour, while the innovative machines currently produce 20,000 pouches per hour. NIPL was the first to develop Stand-up pouches- and Bendable pouches-producing machines for Nestle. The company has the technology to produce machines for products where the product temperature is raised to 130 degrees to kill bacteria and then cooled before packing. It has specialty pouches for products like Lays wafers and many such differentiating products.

Technological advancement and development have proved to be a strong differentiation for NIPL.

Strategic restructuring
Over the years, the company has learned the tricks of the trade and has been restructuring to suit the ever-changing business conditions and customer preferences.

Products

As stated before, ongoing modernization and improvement in the quality of products based on reliable R&D proved to be a backbone for NIPL's success, despite intense competition from multinationals. The company was then looking for a joint-venture partner to enlarge the product base at a separately located 28 acres of land kept ready for such expansion. NIPL is aware that many European owners in their late sixties are looking for disinvestment and sale of their technology and has shortlisted industries for future expansion in machine tools, energy, or electricals.

Processes

NIPL has restructured the processes and has the capability to deploy management techniques like "Six Sigma" to deliver near-perfect products, control inventory levels to the optimum, reduce the assembly time of machines to 8 days against the industry average of around 15 days, and develop the unique advantage of readily having 135 designs to suit an equal number of technically and chemically different products.

HR

HR practices were continuously upgraded to include the following:

- Offering opportunities to all employees for suggesting improvements in productivity and product design
- Providing dignity and respect to all; developing a sense of ownership and freedom of expression
- Initiating free communication channels
- Establishing transparent performance appraisals
- Developing trust

Retiring and loyal employees were encouraged to bring in their new generation as vendors to supply semi-finished goods to NIPL, by providing financial and technical assistance. This move ensured quality, reliability, and regularity in the supply of raw material to NIPL.

Organization

The ability to restructure has been evident from the fact that the company withstood a bitter separation from the joint-venture partner Tetra-pack, a multinational company, due to their arm-twisting attitude. Also NIPL managed to delink from the costly marketing arrangement with Voltas and successfully launched its own marketing setup. Despite such upheavals, the company continued to progress at a CAGR of around 28% and is recognized as a reliable source for all kinds of packaging solutions.

The ability to restructure as per the changing market compulsions enabled NIPL to become a major global player in the packaging industry.

Market leadership

NIPL has been the undisputed leader in the Indian Packaging Industry with twenty-five percent of the market share with a CAGR of twenty-eight percent. It supplies machines to the Dairy industry, Tea industry, Grain and Seeds sector, Snacks, Confectionaries, and the Spices industry. Its major rivals, Samarpan Packaging and Bosch India, have twenty-two and eighteen percent of the market share respectively, and the rest of the market is taken care by smaller manufacturers. However, the planned strategic preparedness along with differentiating factors is capable of increasing NIPL's market share beyond thirty five percent. The intended joint-venture or acquisition would enable NIPL to become a global supplier.

NIPL's last five years' average performance reveals that EBITDA is around 10% against the industry average of 7 to 8%. The availability of land for expansion and fully depreciated utilities further reduces overheads and provides the highest profitability in the packaging industry.

NIPL has the prestigious multinational, NESTLE, regularly buying their machines. NIPL is the only approved SME company for supplies to National Dairy Development Corporation (NDDC) for their all-India requirements. NIPL is the only company in this industry having the capability and technology to produce packaging machines for both solid and liquid products, whereas all other rival companies have a presence in either solid or liquid packing machines. This has given NIPL market leadership in both product segments.

Finolex Cables Ltd. (FCL)
Nature of business
FCL, the first ISO 9001 cable company, has been the pioneer in the manufacture of electric and telephone cables at Pimpri MIDC from way back - from 1958. The range of products produced by FCL includes domestic wires; telephone cables; high tension (HT) power cables; 3 core flat winding wires; optical fibers; optical cables, including multi-core optic fiber cable, auto cables, Jelly Filled Telephone Cables (JFTC), low-density and high-density cables, co-excel cables, and LAN cables; electrical switches; CFL lamps; copper

rods; cable manufacturing machines; and many more products. FCL has been successful in transforming itself from India's primary electrical company to an Electrical Product Company.

Harvard Business School has recognized FCL as a "Hidden Champion."

The role played by the major differentiators in enhancing the profitability and growth of FCL can be elaborated as follows:

Strategic restructuring

FCL's strategy behind successful growth has been the ongoing SWOT analysis, helping the company to reassess its strengths and weaknesses with reference to the changing competition, both local and international; understanding changes in customer preferences; and regularly modernizing machines and utilities. This exercise has also enabled the company to tap new opportunities and minimize the threats coming from both proximate and peripheral boundaries.

Products

The repositioned R&D department assists in making in-house chemical compositions to cover copper cables with a coating to prevent them from rusting and prevent electric shock to users. FCL is the first company to invent and manufacture wiring with PVC coating. Such wires are used in submerged water pumps. FCL was the first company in India to produce jelly-filled telephone cables (JFTC). FCL was also the first to produce halogen-free or fire-free cables; such cables do not catch fire but only produce smoke and cut the electric supply. FCL's network of 21 branches and 3000 channel partners actively feed product information on changing requirement patterns and check for duplicate products that spoil the company's brand.

Processes

The superbrand FCL is known for using innovative technologies to improve processes. The in-house manufactured machines come with specially invented techniques to increase the speed and reduce wastage. Owing to technological developments, the switches manufactured by the company are more lasting and safer to use. The "First-time right" culture ensures improved productivity and reduces waste under conscious monitoring and strict quality checks.

FCL has developed a seamless interdepartmental connect through weekly cross-functional meetings.

Marketing

Market leadership is established with the ever-increasing loyal customer base and best quality of products, giving recognition to FCL as a Super Brand. FCL today controls 40% of the market share in house wiring, 28% in LD wires, and 25% in OFC (optic fiber cables). In a short period of its existence in HD cables, the company has already captured over 12% of the market share. FCL also has more than 10% revenue coming from exports to Europe, the Middle East, and African regions.

HR

Teamwork and intrapreneurship are promoted and encouraged throughout the organization. As an example, the VP (Accounts), conducts monthly meetings for his department where a discussion is held on how to improve their functioning. Morale and motivation are achieved through transparent policies, open annual appraisals, and rewards & recognition of exceptional employees. FCL has a policy to send engineers to collaborators and joint-venture partners to learn new technologies and their applications. Management experts like C. K. Prahalad are engaged to exclusively train senior executives. The Management believes and supports this philosophy: To excel, one has to apply a hands-on approach to his own powerful vision, absorbing various lessons at each step.

Organization

FCL has been restructuring the organization to take care of the expanded activities at regular intervals. To this end, it has been taking many initiatives: practicing Six Sigma for quality production; testing and introducing innovative products; maintaining the highest after-sales services; believing and practicing ethical business; establishing an effective supply chain by ensuring the accuracy of the demand chain (market) through its 2000 SKU's (Stock Keeping Units); linking production and purchases through the Replenishment Method, which is usually followed by FMCG companies, based on the monthly sales plan.

Creativity and Ability of the Management

The quality of strategizing is seen from FCL's transforming its image and scope of the business from a mere Cabler to becoming an Electric Product Company. The thoughtful expansion enabled the company to become a multi-product company in its core expertise area, with the best profitability benchmarked with competitors. Starting from all types of cables, FCL eventually went for backward integration in the manufacturing of copper rods (raw material for copper cables) and fiber (raw material for fiber optic cables) and further diversified into making LED lamps & electrical switches.

In the Indian SME context, the company believes that the implementation of any strategy is unique. Employees in general are not self-motivated, but they obey the directives diligently. That's why FCL successfully practices and ensures job rotation. The spirit of freedom to talk to the top management is nurtured, and good employees are recognized and promoted.

The quality of strategizing is seen from the company's transformation of its image and scope with clarity in assessing how the future market is shaping and knowing global developments and happenings. In this connection, becoming self-sufficient for its electricity needs and going for the in-house solar energy plant was a masterpiece in gaining sustainable competitive advantage.

FCL was considering consolidation of capacities within India and was actively looking at global acquisitions to grab the new market by going for the manufacture of circuit-breaking switches in the first year, electrical fans and industrial motors in the next year, and electrical high voltage Submersible Pumps the following year. FCL is also looking forward to expand the lighting business operations, with the next step being eco-friendly illumination. Clarity of future in strategizing is considered the hallmark of creativity, as exhibited by FCL.

Cost efficiency

Cost efficiency comes from a variety of prudent decisions implemented by FCL:

1. Backward integration to produce the major raw materials - in-house production of copper rods and optic fiber
2. Reduction of interest costs and bad debts by following the Cash Sale policy
3. Modernizing the production capacity with state-of-the-art machinery
4. Policy of just-in-time for procurement of raw material
5. Introducing SAP, an integrated ERP system, to effectively interlink all departments, plants, and stockists, which enables the Replenishment Method for the finished goods (online, backward planning for multiple production units), together with the correct forecast of market requirements, accurate production, and adequate stocking at 20,000 dealers and stock-keeping units (SKUs), to ensure uninterrupted supply of FCL's products to customers
6. Implementing management techniques such as Kaizen and benchmarking
7. Use of Vehicle Tracking System for delivering company's products
8. Fully controlled in-house pricing mechanism for the volatile copper, based on the London Metal Exchange (LME) pricing

Many such effective decisions were implemented to remain cost-effective in the competitive market. Various cost measures stated above ensure that FCL continues to make an average Net Profit of 4%, which is one of the best in the Cable industry, and keeps growing handsomely with a CAGR of around 22%.

Anusaya Auto Pvt. Ltd. (AAPL)

Nature of business

The promoter, Shri. D. T. Wadhokar, is only an ITI graduate (semi-skilled worker). He was working in the tool room of Kirloskar Oil Engines Ltd. (KOEL) as a fitter for eight years. In 1968, he left the job and started a workshop in his house with two hand presses to manufacture washers for KOEL. His skill and dedication earned him a reputation, and more business was generated. In 1978, he expanded his activity at MIDC, Chinchwad, and added pipe bending and pipe assembly manufacturing for Tata Motors. In 1996, the company became Private Limited.

Currently, the company manufactures many auto accessories with an annual turnover of INR 150 crores and supplies to OEMs (original equipment manufacturers). The company holds the Certificate for Quality Manufacturing under ISO 9002 and QS. The company's third manufacturing facility became functional in 2009 at Rudrapur (Uttaranchal).

The role played by the major differentiators in enhancing the profitability and growth of AAPL can be elaborated as follows:

Market Leadership

As an OEM supplier, the firm has unique leadership in producing best quality Auto Sheet Metal components for both, passenger cars, where it controls 80% of the market share, and commercial vehicles, where it controls 40% of the market share.

AAPL also uses timely supply to OEMs as a differentiator to gain and sustain leadership in the competitive market.

Quality of the firm's strategy-making process

From a modest beginning with 2 hand presses to manufacture washers for KOEL to becoming an INR 100 crores plus company, one needs to have a high quality of strategy-making to excel in the chosen field with modest resources. The management of the company was well aware of their limited resources and gradually grew from a house garage to three manufacturing units.

Having established its presence in auto spares, the company in 2009 successfully diversified into supplying components for earth moving equipment and tractor parts for JCB and SAME Auto, based out of Chennai.

Market understanding and quality conscious management have proven their merit in strategy-making and implementation.

Innovations

As a supplier to OEMs, AAPL is expected to innovate not in products but in their own processes to manufacture quality products at affordable cost.

The company has been innovative in its niche segment of technical components, which is a critical part of the assembly. Hands-on experience and skill of management enabled them to innovate in processes, and this is not imitable by the competitors.

Long time association with certain OEMs has also been a source to understand innovative components introduced internationally, which AAPL is able to indigenize in their own unique way.

Praj Industries Ltd. (PIL)
Nature of business

From a modest entrepreneurial venture four decades ago, Praj has become India's leading company in bio-based technologies and engineering, with a strong global presence. Starting as a supplier of ethanol plants, Praj has emerged as a global pioneer, offering an extensive portfolio of sustainable solutions, including bioenergy, high-purity water systems, critical process equipment, breweries, and industrial wastewater treatment technologies. In 1984, the partnership firm was changed to a Private Limited Company in the name of PIL. Today, PIL, an ISO 9001-2000 company, is a founding member of Global Growth companies, a World Economic Forum initiative. PIL operates in Biofuels, which has been acknowledged as a proven alternative to fossil fuels like petrol (gasoline) and diesel when it comes to transportation.

PIL has been creating innovative technology platforms to make biofuels a sustainable and attractive choice. Apart from making agro-linkages stronger, biofuels work toward the mitigation of greenhouse gases for cleaner, greener environment. PIL has become one of the largest resource bases deployed in the industry toward the cause of environment.

PIL also has noteworthy presence in the Brewery industry for engineering and equipment for beer production. In 1994, PIL went public with the issue oversubscribed 7 times. PIL got into technical collaboration with Vogelbusch (Austria) for continuous fermentation process and developed the first innovative product called SPRANNOHILATOR, a zero-pollution system for the treatment of distillery effluents. PIL set up the R&D center dedicated to Ethanol technology. Recognized by GOI's DSIR, this center is equipped with analytical and instrumental laboratory and fermentation, distillation, and effluent treatment pilot plants. The company undertook in-house development of non-molasses technology and engineering for grains and tubers for the first time in India. At the same time, PIL also drew up a plan to diversify into synergistic fields like Brewery Engineering and Plate Heat Exchangers. In 1995, PIL spread its wings in the global market with Praj Far East PTE Ltd. at Singapore. In 2001, PIL tied up with Delta T Corp, USA, for Vapor Phase Molecular Sieve Dehydration plants for production of fuel-grade ethanol. In 2002, PIL entered the East Europe with an engineering order for a grain-based plant. In 2003, PIL launched Multi-feed & Multi-product Ethanol technology for round the year distillery operation. In 2004, PIL entered the Australian market with green-field Fuel Ethanol Production Plant, followed by the launch of Matrix – an innovation center for advanced applied research in the field of ethanol and brewing process in 2005.

In 2006, PIL attained leadership in fuel ethanol plants in India with over 70% market. In 2007, PIL received the ICORE award for leadership in biofuels. During 2011 and 2013, the export oriented unit was established at Markal near Pune, where production of Brewery Mash Filters was started to expand in Brewery Business. In 2014, the fifth Manufacturing facility in Kandla (SEZ), India, was commissioned for bioethanol and biodiesel manufacturing units.

Today, PIL has over 450 references in more than 45 countries across 5 continents with its own offices in Bangkok, Johannesburg, and Sharjah, apart from India. PIL also has a wholly owned subsidiary in USA called Praj Schneider, an engineering firm active in biofuels industry. PIL has set up a Joint-Venture in Europe with Aker Solutions, called BioCnergy Europa B.V., and had another JV recently in Brazil, called Praj Jaragua Bioenergia S.A.

The role played by the major differentiators in enhancing the profitability and growth of PIL can be elaborated as follows:

Innovations

PIL's foremost differentiator over the last more than three decades has been innovations and the development of new technologies.

PIL started as an agro-based processing industry with the first innovative product called SPRANNOHILATOR, a zero-pollution system for treatment of distillery effluents. Since then, the company has focused on core technologies and commissioned many grain-based ethanol plants in India and Europe. The next innovative product was Vapor Phase Molecular Sieve Dehydration plant for the production of fuel grade ethanol.

PIL later launched the multi-feed & multi-product ethanol technology for round-the-year distillery operation and entered the

Australian market with the green-field Fuel Ethanol Production Plant. Currently biofuels form around 5% of the transport fuel mix, and 1% increase in the cost of transport fuel mix translates into 20% increase in the biofuel demand.

PIL launched Matrix – an Innovation Center for advanced applied research in the field of ethanol and brewing process, which assisted the in-house development of non-molasses technology and engineering for grains and tubers for the first time in India. At the same time, PIL also drew up a plan to diversify into synergistic fields like Brewery Engineering and Plate Heat Exchangers.

The company has prepared a counter strategy to maintain its dominance and has formed a team headed by the Senior Management to review each of these action plans, including waste elimination and improvement of business processes that will result in hardcore savings.

Market leadership

PIL's biofuel-based product mix has earned a worldwide reputation of being a one-stop solution in alcohol technology. PIL addresses the entire value chain for processing of alcohol and ethanol-based products and controls 70% of the Indian market share. 50% of the company's sales turnover has been coming from exports, confirming its status as the Market Leader.

PIL's order books are busy with different business lines, viz. alcohol/fuel ethanol plants, biodiesel plants, brewery plants, bionutrients, customized engineering, and manufacturing and agri services. The limited competition comes mainly from KBK Industries and Mojj Industries, respectively controlling 20% and 5% of the market share.

PIL has earned the Super Brand image and has become a world leader in their chosen field by successfully integrating multiple technologies.

PIL has been maintaining EBITDA at around 19% and PAT of around 16%, which compares well with the industry's average at less than 10%.

Creativity and ability of management
The quality of the firm's strategy is evident from the fact that they have consistently excelled in their core business.

The management of the company has been consciously and successfully integrating multiple technologies with the help of the in-house Research and Development wing, which has proven to be the backbone of their success story.

In line with the changing business environment, PIL started an export-oriented unit at Markal near Pune. The company has been judiciously expanding in various backward areas by taking advantage of tax rebates. PIL's fifth manufacturing facility came up in the SEZ zone near Kandla.

The Management at PIL has been learning from past mistakes and consistently supporting on-job learning to transform itself to face the emerging challenges. At opportune times, PIL also formed joint ventures and went in for technical collaborations in their core areas to become a global player.

Talented workforce has been the backbone of the company. It is evident that the spirit of intrapreneurship and teamwork has always been a priority for PIL. In fact, to promote the spirit of intrapreneurship, the Chairman has taken an initiative to offer "MAHA intrapreneurship" award every year to a deserving employee selected from across industries in Maharashtra.

The company's growth has not been steady for the contrasting political stand taken by the countries of the world on alternative fuel energy. However, PIL's committed management was confident that renewable energy is here to stay and that PIL's technological advancement in biofuels would enhance its competitiveness in the longer-term plan. The company has also been exploring other organic and inorganic growth prospects. Despite this limitation, PIL's creative management has managed to consistently grow at 16% CAGR in the last decade.

Warade Industries Pvt. Ltd. (WIPL)
Nature of Business
Warade group of industries was set up in 1989 with a simple but focused mission: "To be first company of choice, by delivering excellent quality products on time and at competitive cost."

WIPL today is a leading manufacturer of Automotive Metal Pressing Accessories like Seat frames, Press tools, Compression molds, Welding jig-fixtures, Panel checkers, Pressure die casting (PDC) tools, and Pressure die casting components. In 2002, WIPL received ISO 9001 certification and in 2005, achieved TS 16949 certification.

WIPL has also been a leading Engineering Services provider and Product Developer of high-end services such as CAD/CAM/CAE, Engineering Designs, Reverse Engineering, Prototype, and Power Coating in the automotive, rail, and manufacturing sectors.

The role played by the major differentiators in enhancing the profitability and growth of WIPL can be elaborated as follows:

Cost Effectiveness

WIPL produces products in the most economically managed operations by way of close monitoring of processes, effective corrections at each stage of production, reducing cycle-time, and minimizing material wastages while the work is in progress. The cost further reduces because the company has developed in-house facilities for all its product range, viz. tool designing, tool manufacturing and pressing, and fabrication.

Cost as a differentiator has enabled the company to generate positive EVA (NOPAT – WACC) in the last seven years of operations despite fierce competition.

Quality of the firm's strategy-making process

WIPL was conscious about supplying quality products and has successfully installed one of the best Tool Rooms at Pune. With the fully-equipped Tool Room supported by able engineers and craftsmen, the company is able to supply high-end products such as Press Dies, Skin Panel Dies, Compression and Injection Moulds, Aluminum pressure Die Casting, Thermal Compression Moulds, Welding Fixtures, Panel Checkers, Automotive Seat Frames, and Sheet Metal Works.

Despite modest resource availability with WIPL (family-owned company), the company grew steadily with quality products and a judicious strategy, which enabled the company to have most of the OEMs in automotive field as their customers. To minimize the risk of over exposure to only car/ truck manufacturing, the company thoughtfully diversified in supplying quality products to the Rail Corporation.

With WIPL's presence in products such as sheet metal and fabrication, which are an integral part of every automobile, and its presence in Die Designing, which has increasing demand, the company has positioned themselves well for sustainable growth trajectory. WIPL has invested in 5 acres of land at Chakan MIDC to take care of expanded activities due to many foreign OEMs planning to set up manufacturing base in India.

WIPL had planned to expand in South and North India to cater to OEMs like Maruti Suzuki, Hero Honda, Honda Motors, and Hyundai. WIPL has come a long way with growing satisfied customer list and is now poised to become a global player.

Effective implementation of strategic processes had enabled the company to control 40% of the market share, followed by the major rival, Harshal Pressing Pvt. Ltd., with 30% and the remaining market catered by smaller companies.[10]

NuLife Pharmaceuticals Ltd. (NPL)
Nature of business
NPL is a pharmaceutical products manufacturing company and is located at MIDC Pimpri, Pune.

The Mission statement of the company is, "Emerge as quality producer, visible, competitive and committed member of global

---

10 The analysis about the companies in the case studies is based on the questionnaire completed by Executive MBA students working in the respective organizations.

healthcare industry. Be seen and felt as highly ethical organization, and one devoted and committed to customer service, customer satisfaction and social responsibility. Emerge as one of the benchmarked companies in the healthcare industry."

NPL is in manufacturing formulations of tablets, capsules, liquid, oral, and external preparations such as ointments, creams, and lotions. NPL holds the necessary drug manufacturing licenses from Maharashtra State. The staff employed by NPL is responsible for manufacture of drugs and trained to maintain the highest standard of Good Manufacturing Practices (GMP). The company was honored with the Industrial Safety Performance Awards in 1990, 91, 92, and 93.

In 1995, NPL received the CAG Award for packaging, and in 1997, it was honored with the Rajiv Gandhi National Quality Award.

NPL currently manufactures 55 products in the area of ENT, Dermatology, Pediatrics, and Ophthalmic formulations and products. A few products of the company are brand leaders in the country.

The role played by the major differentiators in enhancing the profitability and growth of NPL can be elaborated as follows:

Market Leadership

Though NPL has only one Sales office in Mumbai, the company's products are effectively sold in 14 states of India through Consignee Agents. NPL's production facilities comply with the WHO standards. This enables the company to export its products, viz., Soliwax, Gamascab and Salactin, to the highly sensitive American and European markets.

NPL has decided to go beyond the current market space and has drawn ambitious plans for having a national presence. The company also plans to further expand in the existing US and European market, together with entering into the South-East Asia market.

The well-known brand NPL, with the WHO approval, supported by top-line of INR 200 million and a comparable net margin of six percent, has established its position as a Market Leader in the chosen range of drugs.

Innovations

Strong R&D support has enabled NPL to carve out a niche market in a competitive market space dominated by multinational companies. NPL has achieved this through quality products and ongoing innovations, duly supported by the Management.

Drug manufacturing multinationals have specialized in only one of the product groups. For example, Glenmark holds 60% market share in Dermatology products, whereas Bell Pharmacy holds 35% of market share in Ophthalmology products. However, NPL has the innovative advantage of being present in a diverse product range covering ENT, Dermatology, Pediatrics, and Ophthalmic. NPL's leadership in three products, along with low cost of operation and healthy margin, permits NPL to make resources available for innovative products.

NPL had planned to expand in the Ayurvedic drugs market with in-house innovation support to achieve sustainable competitive advantage.

Ability and Creativity of Management

NPL's Chairman Mr. Trivedi, a marketing expert with an international exposure, the CEO, a pharmacist, supported by a couple of directors who were medical practitioners, make a formidable combination to provide technical and market knowledge to expand in the company's core competencies. Despite being in a business, which is predominantly controlled by multinationals, NPL has been growing at CAGR of 14%.

The management at NPL has been prudent to understand the importance of R&D and has accordingly provided sufficient resources.

The delicate task of growth and earning sufficient margin to fuel further growth has been well managed by the management. They grew in their core competitive field and spread the risk to expand in a diverse product range covering ENT, Dermatology, Pediatrics, and Ophthalmic.

The Management's dedication and creativity have enabled the company's products to be recognized by WHO and penetrate the highly sensitive American and European markets.

NPL's management has shown awareness of the new trend, shaping "Style Drugs" in psychotropic, cardiac, and diabetic segments along with biotechnology development. NPL's R&D has been active for the last couple of years and is confident to turn out 2 or 3 patented drugs in this field.

Ayurvedic medicines, which enjoy recognition and acceptance by the masses, the government, and medical professionals, have already been planned by the management, and those formulations will be marketed in the next couple of years.

The ability and creativity of this SME company were established by penetration into advanced markets, by sensing the future market in style drugs, and by focusing on Ayurvedic medicines for sustainable growth.

Vega Controls Pvt. Ltd. (VCPL)
Nature of Business

VCPL is a manufacturer of analog DC drives, value-engineered solutions for various applications, power electronics applications, and IT embedded controls. The company was established in the year 1992. VCPL has achieved remarkable growth due to excellent product quality and committed after-sales service. To efficiently serve growing global customers, VCPL has opened Support Centers in the Middle East and the Far East. The company's market has spread all over India, Middle East, the Far East, and Jordan.

VCPL's unified engineering excellence activity was for a wide range of plant applications in Steel, Paper, Glass, Rubber, Plastic conversion, and in Copper plants. VCPL also offers turnkey solutions for Tier II and Tier III industries to achieve cost-effective automation. VCPL was rated the best performer in the drives and automation field.

The role played by the major differentiators in enhancing profitability and growth of VCP can be elaborated as follows:

Business Process Management (BPM)
Effectively deployed Business Process Management (BPM) at VCPL allows for solving complex problems in the entire life cycle of products from design-to-execution-to-continuous improvement in the company's products and services. It also strengthens internal linkages among different laboratories and departments. Efficient BPM has enabled VCPL to retain its niche market space for more than two decades and has helped to retain the profit margin in the range of 15 to 18 percent, better than the industry average of 12 to 14 percent.

BPM at VCPL also enhances the ability of MIS Reporting and ERP System utilization to support operations to minimize wastage. Effective utilization of such management tools is imperative, particularly when the firm operates both in product manufacturing, contributing 75%, and high-end service providers, contributing the balance 25% of the sales turnover.

VCPL's modern infrastructure and dust-free shop floor ensure that production wastage is kept at negligible levels and enable the company to have higher productivity.

Innovations
The highly specialized product technology differentiates VCPL from its competitors. The range of high-tech products of the company includes analog DC drives, value-engineered solutions for various applications, power electronics applications, and IT-embedded controls. The manufacturing range covers Drives – Thyristor Controlled DC Drivers up to 500 HP and Heater Controllers up to 1000 KW; Smart Interfaces – Tension Controllers, Position

Loop Controllers, and RS 485 and CAN bus interfaces; and System Integration Range – Low & medium voltage AC Drives, Digital DC drives, Automation products, and SCADA Portals.

The creativity and ability of the tech-savvy apex team ensure continued innovations to stay up-to-date with the latest global technological advances. Innovations take two forms in VCPL: The first deals with improvising existing products and processes, and the second curve of innovation deals with new tech products.

The niche market space was fully captured by VCPL due to innovative and better products coming to the market at regular intervals, allowing VCPL to establish a sustained competitive advantage for more than two decades. ABB, a multinational giant, has offered a channel partnership to VCPL for their high technical standards; such recognition not only certifies technical innovativeness but also recognizes effective implementation.

The market trends suggest that future growth for VCPL would emerge from the Power Sector and the Paneling business – PCC & MCC. The company is confident to capture OEM business due to its unique advantages such as a proven track record of minimum resolve time, innovative and latest technology, cost-effective solutions, prompt commissioning, and capable after-sales service.

Management Tools & Techniques

VCPL follows Six Sigma for delivering near-perfect products and services to support the company's balanced portfolio of both, Products Division, contributing 75% to sales turnover, and Engineering Services, contributing 25%.

Management at VCPL has been practicing Co-Learning with their key techno-savvy executives and has been using Benchmarking technique to compare with the best in the world. VCPL's modern infrastructure and dust-free shop floor ensure high productivity and low wastage of raw-material and effective process-time in highly sophisticated and advanced technological products and services. It also enables the company to enhance its core competencies.

Usage of the said management techniques and tools provided CAGR growth to VCPL at 17 percent against the industry average of 14 percent.

For future growth, VCPL has prepared itself to tap the growing need for its products and services in the Power Sector and Steel Plants to maintain sustained competitive advantage.

VCPL, with its said differentiators, is fully equipped to maintain its 20 percent market share despite competition from multinationals, viz., Siemens, SSD Parker, and Rockwell, respectively controlling fifteen, twelve, and seven percent of the market. VCPL, with a current turnover of INR 370 Million and with sizeable surplus, has an opportunity to expand through an IPO (Initial Public Offering) or the joint-venture/acquisition route.

Serum Institute of India Ltd. (SIIL)
Nature of Business
SIIL was established in the year 1966. SIIL is in the business of manufacturing life-saving immunobiological medicines and vaccines at facilities situated in Pune. SIIL has state-of-the-

art manufacturing facilities for the production of vaccines and pharmaceutical formulations. Its manufacturing facilities comply with the international standards of USFDA and WHO.

The company has the capacity to produce over 100 million doses of the HIB vaccine. This product received a good response, and now SIIL supplies this new-age HIB vaccine to international agencies like GAVI (Global Alliance for Vaccines and Immunization), PAHO (Pan American Health Organization), and UNICEF. In the 1980s, for the first time in the world, SIIL collected equine serum by simultaneous and continuous plasmapheresis using IBM Computerized Cell Separator. SIIL gained a technological breakthrough first time in the world to manufacture a Quadruple Vaccine. SIIL's other successful indigenously made products are the Rubella vaccine, DTP-HB, combination vaccine – SIIQ-VAC, DTP-HB-HIB vaccine, and Penta vaccine.

 SIIL has established itself as one of the world's largest producers in the bio-spectrum industry.

The role played by the major differentiators in enhancing the profitability and growth of ALP can be elaborated as follows:

Innovations
Innovation has been the foremost differentiator since the birth of SIIL, which enabled the company to scale its height in an internationally competitive market space.

Reliable and innovative products of SIIL have a stamp of approval from almost all the world's controlling bodies such as GAVI,

PAHO, UNICEF, WHO, and many others. As a result, as of date, sixty percent of the company's sales come from exporting the drugs to over 130 countries in the world.

Some of the notable innovations have been the pilot production of measles vaccine on human diploid cells, industrial column chromatography and affinity chromatography for separation of immunoglobulins, monitoring of quality vaccines in the field, clinical trials of new products, and clinical trials of human diploid cell rabies vaccine.

SIIL has established its credentials by providing quality vaccines like HIIB to global healthcare agencies, thereby reducing the mortality rate due to diseases like measles and others.

Indigenously developed vaccines have a lower R&D cost and lower production cost as compared to multinationals and allow SIIL to deploy large resources to the R&D activity.

Market Leadership
Market leadership of SIIL is established by the fact that 2 out of every 3 children in the world are vaccinated by vaccines produced by the company, and SIIL has also been in the world leadership position as far as MMR and Hepatitis-B vaccines are concerned.

Currently, the rival Indian pharmaceutical companies have been taking the path of global collaborations through mergers and acquisitions. Panacea Biotech, the second largest vaccine producer in India, signed an agreement with PT BioPharma, Indonesia, to manufacture the measles vaccine. In line with the industry trend, SIIL has entered into an agreement with Akron, USA, for definitive developments and exclusive distribution rights for rabies monoclonal antibodies in India and Asian countries. Akron has also agreed to provide funds for product development through various milestones such as the successful completion of Phase I, II, and III of critical trials, leading to eventually receiving CBER approval for the BLA license.

SIIL has the strength and is willing to consider more M&A possibilities for strategically suitable expansion. Market Leadership enabled SIIL to register a handsome PAT of 32% (based on the last seven years' average), and the company's growth at 21% CAGR, the highest in this industry, provides sustainable competitive advantage.

Quality of the firm's strategy-making process

The biotech industry in India mainly consists of five distinct segments: bio-pharmacy, bio-agriculture, bio-industrial, bio-informatics, and bio-services. BioPharma segment, in which SIIL operates, accounts for over two-thirds of the industry and is growing at twenty percent CAGR.

Effective strategic initiative is seen from the actions of the management such as the following:

1. Making resources available for uninterrupted innovations
2. Establishing an autonomous R&D center as early as 1977
3. Expanding in core businesses
4. Keeping high productivity and low cost of production through imparting learning for skill upgradation

5.   Going for Mergers and/or Acquisitions in strategically critical areas

6.   Keeping an eye on the market to assess if either immunity or allergies are getting developed for the company's existing products, and if so, developing new products

7.   Ploughing back sufficient funds to support ongoing research and innovation

8.   Setting up Serum Bio Pharm Park, India's first biotech Special Economic Zone (SEZ) in Pune

Successful operational results spanning over four decades, crossing sales turnover of INR 10,000 million with handsome profits, timely made strategic alliance with Akron, USA, and many more such initiatives certify effective Strategy Making Process.

Auto Line Pvt. Ltd. (ALP)

Nature of Business

The company is in auto-component manufacturing and supplying of components and sub-assemblies required by leading automobile manufacturers. The company started in 1991 as a partnership firm. The OEMs buying the range of ALP's products include parts for two-wheelers, commercial vehicles, three-wheelers, tractors, and passenger cars, thus covering the whole range of automobile OEMs.

The company had a modest beginning on 3000 sq. ft. of production bay at MIDC, Chinchwad. Today it has grown to three factories at Chinchwad, Kudalwadi, and at Chakan, with more than 150,000 sq. ft. of production area. ALP's Chakan and Bhosari units have the ISO/TS 16949: 2002 certification from TUV (rh), Germany, thereby ALP becoming the first Indian SME company to receive this quality certification. In 2006, ALP acquired 51 percent of Dimensions Engineering Software Services Pvt. Ltd. specializing in CAD/CMA/CAE & design engineering services, making ALP a "Concept-to-Delivery" company.

The company has set up a joint venture unit in the UAE to cater to the Gulf and African markets. ALP has since repositioned to manufacture a variety of products/ services including Design Engineering, Prototyping, Tool Making, and mass manufacturing of Critical Components. Though ALP initially was only a contract manufacturer of sheet metal components, the range of products offered by ALP now covers sub-assemblies and formed tubular products, such as silencers and exhaust systems, brake shoes, load bodies, and others.

ALP currently has a manufacturing, design, and engineering footprint in India, US, Europe, Australia, and South-east Asia and counts almost all major OEMs as its customers.

The role played by the major differentiators in enhancing the profitability and growth of ALP can be elaborated as follows:

Creativity and Ability of Management

The creativity of the management is evident from their ability to shape the growth story of ALP from a modest beginning (as a Tier III supplier) to become a formidable force with its manufacturing, designing, and engineering footprint well-established in India, the US, Europe, Australia, and South-east Asia.

ALP's well-timed and strategically suitable acquisitions of Dimensions Engineering Software Services, specialized in CAD/

CMA/CAE and design engineering, and Amogh Engineers, manufacturers of Brake Assembly, paved the way for rapid expansion. ALP's acquisition of smaller rival companies (Tier II & III) aided in creating a synergic effect and gave them full control of the market space. The said creativity and ability of the management enabled ALP to clock a sales turnover of INR 3500 million from a modest beginning of INR 1.1 million.

ALP's creative management also took many timely decisions such as the creation of a state-of-the-art Tool Room facility, improvement of the in-house R&D capabilities, encouragement and motivation to employees for learning and upgradation of skill sets, and upgradation of the latest CAD/CMA facilities.

ALP restructured its design and engineering activities to focus on four product areas: (a) Small mechanical assemblies: Jacks and Toolkits, Pedal systems, Door hinges, and others; (b) Body Structures: Fabricated assemblies for Automobile and Engineering industries, Door assemblies, Driver Cabins, Generator-set canopies, and large assemblies for LCVs and passenger cars; (c) Chassis Systems: Fabricated assemblies for underbody and chassis components, axels, and pick-up boxes; (d) Special Purpose and Formed Tubular Products: Exhaust systems, silencers, tubular fabricated assemblies, and specialty fabricated mechanisms.

The said qualities projected by the management would go a long way in improving and sustaining growth and profitability.

Market Leadership

The formidable positioning by ALP in the local as well as international market can be seen from the following:

1. The company has secured 4 patents in the US market, viz. Automobile Quick Jack, Load Body Extender, Spare Tire carrier Winch, and Roto Crank.

2. ALP's reputation as a supplier of quality products makes them the first choice vendor for new incoming auto OEMs in India.

3. ALP's capability of providing "design engineering" and customizing "critical vehicle components" along with "rapid prototyping of components" gives them an edge over competitors.

4. Obtaining "CQ" certification, allowing ALP's products to go directly to OEM's "online" production, without prior inspection, makes the company a unique supplier of components.

In view of the said advantages, ALP has received Letters of Intent for new business from OEMs like Daimler Chrysler, Cummins Power Generation, General Motors, and Volkswagen, empathetically proving the company's market leadership as a major differentiator.

ALP's sustainable competitive advantage will emerge from the above massive export potential worth US$ 40 billion (in 2015) and growth at a CAGR of 17%.

Cost Effectiveness

ALP, through modernization of machinery and operations processes, has achieved economy in cost of production and kept overheads at a minimum to compete with the multinationals.

While the opportunities to grow are plenty, the major challenge comes from fluctuations in the price of steel, the uncertainty of crude prices, and the cyclical "lean period" for automobile sales. The said challenges make net margin low for this industry, and survival and growth depend on how the company achieves economies on the cost front.

ALP shifted from traditional press line to automated transfer of parts to press using robots, usage of KBK rails for "Welding Gun" hanging instead of conventional mild steel shapes beams, commissioning of "walking beam conveyor" for floor assembly, centralized CO_2 gas distribution line to each welding machine, fully automated line of pick and place overhead conveyer, cushion for 800 Ton capacity press that was designed and manufactured in-house, and many more innovations and modernizations. This has helped the company to improve quality and productivity along with a reduction in operations cost by reducing manpower requirements, reducing damages to components, and reducing workmen fatigue.

Cost leadership and competitiveness at ALP are seen from its operating profit or EBITDA of around 28 percent as compared to the industry's average operating profit of 18 to 20 percent. The company has been earning net margin/ PAT @ 5% on average for the last seven years. CAGR in the last seven years has been more than the industry average at 26%.

APLAB Ltd. (APLAB)

Nature of business

APLAB was incorporated in 1962 and is known as a technology-driven company run by professionals. The company is the manufacturer of a wide range of products for Telecommunication, Information, ATMs, Fuel Dispensing, and Power control equipment. The company's products are exported to global customers, and they meet with international standards of safety and reliability such as UL, VDE, etc. The company has four independent product divisions: Test and Measurements equipment, Power Conversion and UPS systems, Self-service Terminals for banking, and equipment for Petroleum sector. The company was awarded ISO 9002 certificate by STQC, Department of Electronics, GOI, which is a recognition for continuous innovation and improvement of quality in their range of products.

The role played by the major differentiators in enhancing the profitability and growth of APLAB can be elaborated as follows:

Creativity and Ability of Management

APLAB's creativity and ability are seen from the way the company has been progressing in the highly technology-oriented product range where multinationals have been dominant players. After incorporation, the company established itself in the market with its own quality products, based on in-house expertise, for almost two decades, after which, in 1990, it diversified into telecommunication test equipment with the first technical collaboration with a Japanese company. Later, at periodical intervals, APLAB signed new collaborations to address the rapidly changing market needs and kept consolidating its position in the expanded product range.

To remain focused on core expertise and to keep an arm's length distance between different collaborators, the management at APLAB formed three separate subsidiary companies catering to different products.

The ability and creativity of the management are also seen from their diluting minority stake in the company through the disinvestment route and using raised resources for acquiring additional electronic products technology (ATMs). Another strategic initiative taken by the management was dividing the Sales/ Marketing function into four regions of India, viz., Western, Eastern, Southern, and Northern regions, and by keeping the manufacturing activity centralized in Pune. Regional sales function reduced advertising and selling overheads to add 2% to the net margin. The company was planning to diversify in IT-related Hardware manufacturing.

Usage of Management Tools and Techniques
APLAB deals with a large range of products spanning from Telecommunication, Information, and ATMs to Fuel Dispensing and Power control. Such a diverse range requires different skill sets. To support this, the company regularly sends their engineers to the headquarters of collaborators for upgradation of skills. The company also spends a lot of money by inviting experts for the upgradation of skills and sending their engineers for refresher courses. Later the trained engineers are required to share their

knowledge within their departments in the workshops organized by the HR department.

APLAB judiciously expanded in the area of their Core Competencies, which enabled the company to grow at CAGR of 12%, which compares well in the erratic market conditions.

As regards the quality of products, financials, and training facilities, APLAB has been benchmarking itself with the multinationals operating in this field. This initiative enabled the company to qualify for supplies to the sensitive Defense Department and establish their imprint in the B2B industrial applications.

Innovations

Operating in the field of Electronic Equipment, APLAB prospered mainly due to Innovations, both in-house and through collaborators. But for innovation, it was unthinkable for an ISO 9002-certified company to survive and grow from the sixties till date in a market that is changing at a supersonic speed, with new applications emerging practically on a daily basis. GOI, too, awarded APLAB for continuous innovations and recognized the company.

The company is a recognized leader in the production of various electronics products such as telecommunication test equipment and battery testing equipment. It launched computer interactive retail petrol pumps and dispensers for the first time in India as well as ALFA petrol station controller along with the software "Indhan," which allows online control of electronic dispensers, and further diversified into high-end Technology products like ATMs for retail banking, along with IT solutions used in the said ATM machines.

The innovation-enabled APLAB controls 15 percent of the market share and has been placed second in the market that is dominated by multinational companies, led by Siemens with 35 percent.

Elite Group of Industries (EGI)
Nature of Business
EGI commenced its business operations in 1973 at Bhosari, Pune. The company is in the manufacturing of molded plastic products for industrial use. At the start of its operation, the company had only one customer - Exide batteries - and registered a small turnover of INR 5 million. Gradually the company expanded in the Injection Molding business. As of date, the group has three subsidiaries, viz. Elite Industries, contributing 50 percent of the turnover; Plastomech Industries, contributing 30 percent; and Borate Plastics, contributing 20 percent of the turnover. In the year 2004, EGI expanded its operations by starting Tool Design and Tool Manufacturing activities.

The role played by the differentiators in enhancing the profitability and growth of EGI can be elaborated as follows:

Implementation of Strategy
EGI gives high weightage to the effective implementation of engineering excellence and close monitoring of high productivity in different types of product groups. The company has created two separate subsidiary companies to effectively

maintain its formidable position in supplying a variety of molded products to the B2B segment companies representing different industries. That effective implementation has enabled EGI to receive the TS 16949 certification, which is rather rare in SMEs.

The company has geared itself to cater to the ever-expanding market by purchasing 5 acres of land at MIDC, Chakan. EGI was also to add VMC and EDM machines to augment their Tool Room facility.

The company had placed an order to purchase molding machines of 650 T and 850 T, which is an integral part in creating the state-of-the-art manufacturing facility at the newly acquired land.

Due to the effective implementation and control, EGI has been receiving many joint venture proposals from multinationals.

Cost Effectiveness

EGI's capability of effective monitoring of operations, minimum wastage in production bay, and regular maintenance of machinery, along with its well-trained workforce, ensure cost effectiveness, which is essential in stiff competition.

Backward integration to mold designing, duly supported by the in-house Tool Room facility, ensures availability of better quality molds. This backup facility enables the company to make quality molds as per customer specifications, in minimum time and at low cost. The company is known to be producing molds at 60%

of the cost in comparison with industry standards. The company has been earning PAT at around 4%, with CAGR of 30%, which compares well with the industry norms.

Cost-effectiveness has enabled EGI to be the best-suited company to expand with the ever-growing automobile and white goods industry and stay profitable despite an increasing number of MNCs entering the plastic molding industry.

Market Leadership

EGI has been a dominant player as a specialty producer for quality industrial plastic products in the growth-oriented B2B segment. The company's product range includes TV covers, seat side valence covers, various types of knobs, battery components, steering columns, pillars, storage bins, armrest mechanisms, crates, and many more products used by OEMs in both blow-molded and injection-molded products.

EGI started with only one specialty machine to supply blow-molded cases to Exide Batteries, a German company, and today it has progressed to be a leading supplier to many large OEMs.

EGI, an ISO 9001 certified company, today is the undisputed leader in the market and is supplying its quality products to many multinationals like Lear Corporation, Mahindra, Visteon, BEHR, Daewoo, LG, National Panasonic, Sharp, TATA, Videocon, and other OEMs.

Rewale Engineering Pvt. Ltd. (REP)

Nature of Business

Rewale Engineering Pvt. Ltd., a diversified manufacturing company, commenced the business in 1991, to manufacture an exhaustive range of generators of all kinds of commercial and consumer usage. REP, an ISO 9001:2000 company, is known for Standard Diesel Genesets and Silent Diesel Genesets manufacturing from 2.5 KVA to 300 KVA capacities. Its DG sets are manufactured under state-of-the-art facilities at their factory in Chakan, Pune.

In less than a decade, Rewale Group of Industries expanded into a variety of products and businesses, viz. Automobile Engineering, Precision Electronics, Electrical Components, Press Parts, Sheet Metal Products, Acoustic Enclosures, Pharmaceuticals, Hotels, and Information Technology. In 2009, REP Group's turnover crossed beyond INR 3000 million, and the net profitability is comfortably around 10 to 12 percent. REP supplies its quality products to global giants like ABB, Thermax, Cummins, Electronica, Airtel, Ericsson, Hutch, and others.

The role played by the major differentiators in enhancing the profitability and growth of REP can be elaborated as follows:

Business Process Management (BPM)

REP started with the manufacture of small size Diesel Generators, and within a decade, the company established its niche market (small size DG sets), both for industry and direct consumers, with 60 percent market share. The company gives high importance to their ability of solving complex problems in the entire life cycle of their products.

Multiple structures adopted by the REP provided good business control and allowed the company to pick up product-specific ERP along with smaller but efficient MIS structures for gaining better internal linkages.

REP's effective Business Processes allowed them to profitably manage a variety of business lines such as Automobile Engineering, Precision Electronics, Electrical Components, Press Parts, Pharmaceuticals, Hotels and Information Technology.

Cost Effectiveness
The company has in-house schemes to encourage its engineers to develop and implement new ideas in the plant, which can improve productivity or reduce per unit cost of production.

The Management supports such initiatives by cash rewards to both, the individual concerned and his team. This practice generates Team Spirit and increases Productivity.

REP's ability to control the cost of production and lower the overheads enables them to offer quality products at a lower selling point in comparison to competitors. REP's net profitability averaging around 10% in the last seven years compares well with the industry average.

Quality of the firm's strategy-making process

REP started manufacturing small size DG sets for industry and consumers. The quality of their products earned them a reputation, and it was awarded with the ISO 9001:2000 certification.

The management realized that with their limited resources, their SME Company cannot compete with multinationals in large size DG range. Wisely, REP decided to manufacture "Acoustic Enclosures" and "Sheet Metal" products, which suited their Core Competency.

The good quality products and reliability of timely supply earned them a good name, and soon, REP's products were accepted by global giants like ABB, Thermax, Cummins, Electronica, Airtel, Ericsson, Hutch, and others.

Eventually, the Management's acumen and core competencies in engineering enabled REP to successfully diversify into a range of business activities such as Automobile Engineering, Precision Electronics, Electrical Components, Press Parts, Pharmaceuticals, Hotels, and Information Technology.

The company's controlled aggression took them from a modest beginning to over INR 3000 million in sales, with CAGR of 14%, showing the quality of the strategy making processes.

Having come to a sizable turnover and with consistently good profitability, the REP group is now at a takeoff stage in technology-oriented engineering products, which is their core competency. REP, with good branding of its own, is planning to grow with suitable joint ventures and/or technical alliances to become a Global Company.

Lokesh Machines Ltd. (LML)
Nature of Business

The company manufactures Special Purpose Machines, CNC General Purpose Machines, machine tools, and automobile components. It has a professional team with rich experience in design, development, production, machine tools, Jigs, Fixtures, and Accessories needed for precision engineering. Since its incorporation in 1983, the company has made its name for quality products and gets 60 percent of its new business from repeat customers. LML's well-knit service setup has trained engineers and craftsmen who give best results backed by state-of-the-art manufacturing facilities. The company has a technical alliance with Grob GmbH, Germany. In the segment of Auto Components, the company has been concentrating on manufacturing and machining auto components for OEMs such as Bajaj Auto, Mahindra and Mahindra, Escorts, Ashok Leyland, Honda, and others for machining Cylinder Box at the plant set up at MIDC, Ranjangaon. In 2006, LML received the Best Exporter Award from the Sir M. Vishveswaraiah Foundation.

The role played by the major differentiators in enhancing the profitability and growth of NPL can be elaborated as follows:

Innovations

The foremost differentiator for LML has been actively sponsoring Innovations and Excellence in Operations. Innovative products and processes have taken the company from its modest beginning to becoming a major supplier to Indian OEMs to supplying the multinational Honda to exporting its products to the quality-conscious European Market, which has been a phenomenal success.

All products of the company, such as Special Purpose Machines, CNC General Purpose Machines, machine tools, and automobile components have acceptance from most of the multinational OEMs.

As a corporate policy, LML extends support for learning and upgradation of skills to its professional team. The motivated team is known to have rich expertise in designing; developing; producing; and handling machine tools, Jigs, Fixtures, and Accessories needed for precision engineering. Such assistance has enabled the company to export CNC Lathes and Vertical Machining Centers to the advanced European market.

Product innovation and process improvements by the company have attracted a German Company to enter into a technical alliance, which has opened up the global market to LML.

LML is the recipient of the best Exporter Award from the Sir M Vishveswaraiah Foundation.

Cost Effectiveness

LML judiciously grew without taking any undue risk in the ever-changing market place, from "license raj" to post 1991, and was mindful of keeping the production cost and overheads minimum while maintaining the product quality benchmarked to the best in the market.

The company has been registering average PAT of 10% and CAGR growth at 11% in the last seven years, which compares well with the industry average.

The ability to differentiate on cost effectiveness is evident from the current EBIDTA of LML at INR 46 Million in comparison with giant companies like Thermax at INR 200 million, Alfa Laval at INR 5 million, and Sulzar India at INR 10 million.

Market Leadership

LML has vertically divided the company as per Product Groups, with each product headed by a qualified Director (non-board member). Thus each product group, viz. Assembly, Innovative Technology, Auto Component, and CNC machines, etc., is a separate Profit Center. Internal competition among different profit centers has led the company to gain leadership in the market despite the presence of multinationals.

LML has an impressive list of satisfied OEMs in India and from the developed world, which proves the global acceptability for the company's products and proves their Market Leadership under the SME category.

LML, the recipient of the "Quality of Management" award, has an in-house training center for workmen and a tie-up with one of the management schools for training middle and senior management teams to retain their edge in marketing.

LML has established a countrywide Dealer Network, which stocks the company's products and assists the marketing team in gaining a larger market share. LML's well-knit service setup has trained engineers and craftsmen who give their best and on-call after-sales service to the customers.

The company was looking for a suitable Joint-Venture partner or is open for Technical Collaboration for expanding its exports.

India Pistons Ltd. (IPL)

Nature of Business

The company has been India's first auto-ancillary venture established in July 1949 at Shiroli MIDC, Pune, to meet the growing requirements of domestic OEM's in automobile sector.

Currently IPL manufactures a range of pistons for heavy duty diesel engines and gas engines. It also has a range of diesel engines for light commercial vehicles, passenger cars, and bi-wheeler (4 stroke) small engine applications.

As the oldest auto-ancillary manufacturer in India today, IPL maintains its pre-eminent position in the domestic automotive market, and IPL's customer base is the recognition of years of uninterrupted and consistent performance. Way back in 1971, IPL developed the Ring Carrier Piston for Cummins as an import substitution. The company has technical collaboration with Sakura Kogyo, Japan, for technical up-gradation. IPL has ISO 9002 certification by BVQI, UK; QS 9000 certification; and TS 16949 certification from TUV, Germany.

IPL continues to build on its successes and the company evolves to meet the requirements of the dynamic marketplace.

The role played by the major differentiators in enhancing the profitability and growth of NPL can be elaborated as follows:

Strategic Restructuring and Disinvestment

IPL has been progressing well in the last more than six decades mainly due to the company's ability to position and reposition itself as required by the ever-changing market conditions and customer demands.

The company made many major decisions in restructuring its business and disinvested from the non-profitable ventures. At the beginning of 2000, the company realized the need for good quality metal for producing world-class aluminum castings, which satisfy the chemical, mechanical, and other metallurgical properties essential for the piston to withstand high temperature and pressure during its operational tenure in the engine. To achieve this objective, IPL went in for backward integration and established its own Aluminum Foundry Plant.

IPL signed a technical collaboration with Sakura Kogyo, Japan, and created a separate profit center to monitor its progress. Later came the technology tie-up with Izumi Industries, Japan, and a separate sub-division was established. To withstand the increasing competition from multinationals, IPL signed the Technical License Agreement with Dong Yang Piston, South Korea, and floated the subsidiary company, India Piston Rings.

Strategically, all plants catering to expanded activities under different collaborations, are located in rural Maharashtra, which provides advantages such as low cost of production, availability of adequate semi-skilled labor force, and low cost of infrastructure.

Many such decisions on restructuring the organization and the way of doing business differentiated IPL and enabled them to meet the dynamic market conditions. As a result, in the last seven years, despite the slowdown, IPL has been registering a CAGR of around 9-10%.

To safeguard from future competition, IPL is open to considering dilution of their equity holding in favor of a suitable joint venture partner. With multinational OEMs coming to India, the company needs the technology corridor, so that in a year or two, the company can have a new technical collaboration.

Innovation

Path-breaking innovations have been one of the important differentiators for IPL. Innovations in product design and production processes have firmly established IPL as a high quality and reliable supplier of precision auto-components to the majority of the OEMs and to discerning customers in the after-market.

IPL simultaneously works on two innovative curves: First, the company improvises the existing products and processes; secondly, it strives to bring in new and more efficient products.

Innovations have earned the company two recognitions, QS 9000 Certification and TS 16949 Certification from TUV, Germany. Six Sigma applications have brought down rejections and have enabled IPL to supply 1.5 million defect-free Pistons to Cummins.

Recently, IPL's in-house R&D developed the "cooled gallery piston for heavy duty application" and joined the group of elite companies from the developed world.

Innovations have enabled IPL to face three main competitors, viz., Samira Pistons & Rings Ltd., ANG Auto Ltd., and Bharat Gears Ltd. However, IPL has a formidable list of many satisfied customers in different business segments, viz., Tata Motors and Suzuki in Automotive, Kirloskar and Eicher in the Tractor industry, and Crompton Greaves and Cummins India in Industrial Applications, providing an edge over rivals and giving assured growth.

Spirit of Intrapreneurship and Teamwork

IPL's success is unthinkable without dedicated "Intrapreneurs" or "Corporate Entrepreneurs," professionals working within the organization who turn ideas into profits and who lead to rapid growth of the company.

IPL's management and HR have been constantly providing motivation and training to upgrade the skillsets of employees. As a team, IPL employees are aware that it is imperative that each of them has both a responsibility and an obligation for performance.

The manufacture of precise auto components needs a faultless process. To avoid any lapse in quality, the whole process, from the purchase of steel-to-machining-to-fitting electronic applications-to-assembly, has to be precisely controlled. IPL has deployed various internal linkages through the effective ERP system to monitor and control precision.

IPL has provided a well-equipped laboratory with a spectrometer and image analyzer apart from other essential checking and quality instruments and equipment, which are complemented by sophisticated Quality Control systems to ensure consistently high-quality piston manufacturing.

Motivated and satisfied employees did provide a major differentiator in IPL's success.

Statistical Inference on Differentiators and their Impact on Increased Profitability / Growth

Research findings of the above live cases revealed that the differentiators work in tandem; however, the importance of each differentiator varies from company to company, depending on the business environment surrounding the particular company. The importance of each differentiator and its contribution to enhance the profitability of the company was based on the opinion and feedback received from the respective company's CEO and Top Management.

Table 9: Comparative Importance of the Differentiators in the Researched Indian Companies

Companies	Premium Transmission	Nichrome	Finolex Cables	Anusaya Auto Pvt.Ltd	Praj	Warade Industries	Nu Life Pharmaceuticals	Vega	Serum	Autoline	APLAB	Elite	Rewale Engineers	Lokesh Machines	India Pistons
	1	2	3	4	5	6	7	8	9	10	11	12	13	14	15
DIFFERENTIATORS	%	%	%	%	%	%	%	%	%	%	%	%	%	%	%
Market Leadership	4	10	10	11	11	9	13	10	12	12	9	11	9	10	7
Innovations	6	13	7	8	13	10	12	11	15	9	9	10	6	13	13
Cost Effectiveness	9	7	10	8	5	12	10	8	8	11	6	12	11	12	9
Business Process Management	9	4	9	7	5	9	6	13	4	8	6	6	13	6	8
Learning & Shared Vision	9	9	6	7	9	8	6	8	4	7	11	6	6	8	7
Quality of firms strategy making process	10	9	9	12	9	11	6	6	11	6	7	9	12	11	7
Usage of Mgmt. techniques & tools	8	8	8	8	10	7	10	9	5	8	13	6	8	6	7
Creativity & ability of Mgmt.	12	11	11	10	11	7	11	8	9	13	12	6	6	6	8
Spirit of Intrapreneurship & teamwork	11	8	4	6	7	7	7	6	7	6	7	6	8	6	8
Implementation of Strategy	9	4	8	8	6	10	6	9	8	6	6	13	6	8	7
Developed peripheral vision	4	5	5	6	5	5	7	6	7	6	8	6	6	6	7
Strategic restructuring & disin-vestments	9	12	13	9	9	5	6	6	10	8	6	9	9	8	12
Total	100	100	100	100	100	100	100	100	100	100	100	100	100	100	100

Statement Showing Companywise Importance of Differentiators

The information received from CEOs with proven track record has brought forth valuable information for applying Statistical Tools and Techniques. These findings were statistically analyzed for greater clarity on their importance in enhancing the profitability of Companies. Firstly, Spearman's Correlation Coefficient was used to clarify, both importance wise and rank wise, whether there is any correlation among various differentiators. Those having high correlation, either positive or negative, were studied for further understanding, and the outcome was analyzed. Secondly, Multiple Regression Analysis was carried out to test the hypothesis to understand the significance of the "Collective Impact" of all differentiators on the profitability of the companies, and the outcome was suitably commented. Lastly, Linear Regression Analysis was carried out to test the hypothesis to understand the significance of the "Individual Impact" of a differentiator on the profitability of the companies, and the outcome was suitably commented.

The outcome of statistical analysis reaffirmed the research findings that collectively, the differentiators have a significant impact on the enhancement of profitability in the said Companies, and they work in tandem. However, individually, none of the differentiators had a significant impact on the profitability of the company.

Conclusion on the Role of Differentiators

Researched companies were found to be using differentiators in their strategy making, which helped them in planning and achieving desired goals, mapping their own progress, and adopting winning strategies suitable to the unique business environment in which they were operating. These processes enabled the companies to position and reposition themselves to withstand competition and meet with changing customer requirements and keep progressing decade after decade.

The importance and relevance of differentiators in impacting profitability was allotted by the CEOs of the respective companies. Select companies and their CEOs have proven track record of growing their business to higher profitability and growth in comparison to the industry average.

The research outcome indicated that the differentiators work in tandem, though a few of them play a major role in the success of the company, depending upon the peculiar business environment in which the company operates. It was also observed that differentiators "collectively" have a positive impact on the performance of the company, but "individually" none of them has a significant impact on the profitability of the company. At the same time, an outcome suggested that each of the twelve differentiators had some role to play in enhancing the profitability and success of the SME Companies.

The management of the said companies used diverse input across functional boundaries, resulting in "ownership and buy-in" of progressive strategies by their employees to make their mission possible. The "collective and participative" approach followed by the said progressive companies created winning teams. Research findings suggested that usage of effective differentiators prepared the company employees to take on big, hairy, and audacious goals (BHAG) and created a crystal clear road map of progress.

Hope the book would guide entrepreneurs and learners in understanding the role of differentiators in different companies operating in a variety of industries and enable them to deploy suitable impactful differentiators in their own companies to achieve enhanced profitability and growth.

Chapter 9
Final Thoughts

In this millennium, we live in interesting times. We stand at the brink of many new opportunities; a world in which rules keep changing – through regulatory compliance, shifting consumer expectations, security threats, and the emergence of new global markets and competition. To be successful in such challenging times, we learned from this book how companies should develop winning teams, draw up dependable strategies and plans, deploy suitable differentiators, and attain "Level-Next".

In Part I, we reviewed the changing business landscape for Indian companies, taking cognizance of global competition in this bold and barrier-less world. Readers were introduced to the evolution of the most powerful concept of Competitive Advantage and understanding of the Generic Strategic Management Process along with some of the most useful and powerful concepts in Business Strategy.

Part II of the book covered how to develop your own Winning Team, capable of defining, shaping, practicing, and implementing the Strategic Process to gain sustainable competitive advantage. Taking a real-life example, we saw how a CEO interacted with managers up to the 5th level, and based on the findings from where the "action is," developed a blueprint of the Action Plan.

He formed and assimilated the "Core Team" to act as a catalyst of change. Later, he addressed the Pain Areas and began developing a meaningful SWOT analysis after which, the need for restructuring the organization was felt. Assessing future readiness further sharpened the Core Team's focus, and a united team with a common goal was ready to draw up a strategic road map of the planned growth.

Based on my experiments conducted in SMEs, a typical time frame of the stages discussed takes about 18 weeks. (Refer to the end note of the Strategic Process, Chapter 6.)

The stage-by-stage approach discussed in the book illustrates the pragmatic ways in which successful companies navigate through the world of strategic management – an extremely complex system of defining, implementing, evaluating, and recreating successful strategies.

Part III concluded that the concept of Competitive Advantage is constantly evolving and remains in a state of paradigm. While differentiation is recognized as a key discriminator, its impact on a company's success is difficult to assess and fully comprehend.

My research revealed the twelve most impactful differentiators deployed by successful Indian companies. The case studies of a few select companies enlightened us about company-wise reliance on each differentiator. Companies that were able to judiciously deploy a Differentiating Strategy were able to stay ahead of the curve. Next, we got familiarized with the fact that the importance of each differentiator in the company's success varies from company to company, depending upon the complex business environment in which each company operates. Each company faces unique challenges and has its own product mix, competitors, employee skill sets, market trends, and various other factors that influence the significance of each differentiator and their combined impact on the company's success. (The interplay of the said variables has been discussed in Chapter 8.)

The innovative approach to understanding the role of differentiators leads us to realize their "Collective Impact" in transforming companies into powerful, smooth-running business enterprises. Differentiators enabled the unleashing of intrapreneurial energy, creativity, and innovation within the ranks and created leadership at different levels for the organization to prosper. The usage of differentiators prepared employees to take on BHAGs (big, hairy, audacious goals) and paved the way to attain "Level Next."

I hope this book provides valuable insights to entrepreneurs and business strategy learners, helping them to achieve long-term success, focus on their most important goals, and stay true to their strategic roadmap while remaining open to new opportunities.

Exhibits

(a) **Exhibits 1 to 4:** Feedback forms for Measuring Work Challenges, Employee Training & Development, Competencies Mapping, and People Management Challenges. (Ref. Chapter 5, under Human Resources Strategic Focus.)

Exhibit 1

Work Challenges:

Listed below in alphabetical order are 5 areas of your Work Challenges. Distribute a total of 10 points among them, according to the weightage they carry in your opinion.

Work Challenge	Points
Managing Customers	
Managing People	
Managing Processes	
Managing Teams	
Managing Technology	
Total	10

(Source: Company's Internal Record)

Exhibit 2

EMPLOYEE TRAINING & DEVELOPMENT

STRENGTHS	AREAS OF IMPROVEMENT

(Source: Company's Internal Record)

Exhibit 3

Sr. No.	Parameter	
A	**Technical and Business Competencies**	
1	Own and Business and Product Line	
2	Environment	
3	Competitors and Their Strategies	
4	Customer and Market	
5	Technology	
6	Finance	

Sr. No.	Parameter	
7	Research and Development	
8	Manufacturing Process	
9	Quality Requirements	
B	**Managerial Competencies**	
1	Short-term Goal Setting	
2	People Management	
3	Customer Management	
4	Union and Associates	
5	Team Management	
6	Technology Management	
7	System Management	
8	Resource Management	
9	Public Relations	
10	Environment Management	
11	Quality and Customer Care	
12	Safety Management	
13	Financial and Cost Management	
14	Boss Management or Managing Seniors	
C	**Leadership or Transformational Competencies**	
1	Articulating and Communicating Mission and Values	
2	Formulating and Managing Strategies or Strategic Thinking	
3	Long-term Planning and Policy Making	
4	Setting Challenging and Achievable Goals	
5	Value and Culture-building	
6	Mobilizing and Creating a Resource Base	

Sr. No.	Parameter	
7	Exploring New Markets and New Technologies	
8	Inspiring and Empowering People	
9	Influencing the Thinking of Seniors, Customers, and Stakeholders	
	OVERALL	

(Source: Company's Internal Record)

Exhibit 4

People Management Challenges

		Very Important	Fairly Important	Least Important
1	Recruiting New Talent			
2	Retaining Talent			
3	Employee Compensation			
4	Developing Internal Leadership			
5	Employee Health			
6	Employee Motivation			
7	Managing Change			
8	Corporate Social Responsibility			

		Very Important	**Fairly Important**	**Least Important**
9	Internal Communication			
10	Outsourcing HR			
	Any other: Please List			

(Source: Company's Internal Record)

Index

About the Author

Kaustubh Medhekar earned his MBA from Jamnalal Bajaj Institute of Management Studies, Mumbai. He did his Ph.D. (Management) from Symbiosis International University, Pune.

Dr. Medhekar is a seasoned management professional with over 30 years of senior-level industry experience, including board room exposure in India and overseas. Later, he shifted to academics and worked as an Associate Professor at Symbiosis Institute of Business Management, Pune.

Currently, he is engaged in 'ConsultMent', (Consulting and Mentoring) for SME segment companies that are willing to learn and adapt progressive strategies to attain Level-Next. He also conducts corporate training in many verticals, such as Business Strategy, Leadership & Team building, and Financial Management. He has been regularly invited as a guest faculty by management institutions to share his views on various contemporary aspects of business.

He has many research papers to his credit in the domain of Business Strategy, and Finance. He has been writing articles in the management journals & magazines.